REREADING LITERATURE
John Milton

REREADING LITERATURE
General Editor: Terry Eagleton

John Milton
Language, Gender, Power

Catherine Belsey

Basil Blackwell

Copyright © Catherine Belsey 1988

First published 1988

Basil Blackwell Ltd
108 Cowley Road, Oxford, OX4 1JF, UK

Basil Blackwell Inc.
432 Park Avenue South, Suite 1503
New York, NY 10016, USA

All rights reserved. Except for the quotation of short passages for
the purposes of criticism and review, no part of this publication
may be reproduced, stored in a retrieval system, or transmitted, in
any form or by any means, electronic, mechanical, photocopying,
recording or otherwise, without the prior permission of the
publisher.

Except in the United States of America, this book is sold subject to
the condition that it shall not, by way of trade or otherwise, be lent,
re-sold, hired out, or otherwise circulated without the publisher's
prior consent in any form of binding or cover other than that in
which it is published and without a similar condition including this
condition being imposed on the subsequent purchaser.

British Library Cataloguing in Publication Data
Belsey, Catherine
    John Milton.——(Rereading Literature).
    1. Milton, John, *1608-1674*——Criticism and interpretation
    I. Title   II. Series
    821'.4   PR3588

    ISBN 0-631-13346-1
    ISBN 0-631-13499-9 Pbk

Library of Congress Cataloging in Publication Data
Belsey, Catherine.
    John Milton / Catherine Belsey.
        p.   cm.——(Rereading literature)
    Includes index.
    ISBN 0-631-13346-1
    ISBN 0-631-13499-9 (pbk.)
    1. Milton, John, 1608-1674——Criticism and interpretation.
I. Title.   II. Series.
PR3588.B37   1988
821'.4——dc 19

Typeset in 11 on 12 pt Baskerville
by Colset Private Ltd, Singapore
Printed in Great Britain by Billing & Sons Ltd, Worcester

To Jennie, Nicholas and Philip
in memory of Richard

Contents

Editor's Preface

Like Shakespeare and Wordsworth, John Milton is something of a national institution, as much a part of the English landscape as fox-hunting or the Bank of England. That this revered, monumental figure clamoured in his own day for the execution of the king, penned heresy, floated close to plebeian radicalism and was fortunate to escape in one piece at the Restoration, are embarrassments which conventional criticism has coped with as best it can. *Comus* is in its own way a radical blast against the Establishment; *Paradise Lost* is a poem built on the ruin of utopian political hopes, and *Samson Agonistes* a dark, tormented text; but it has always been possible to edit out this turbulent history and attend instead to Milton's 'music' and spiritual grandeur. His patriotism, like William Blake's, has been appropriated by some of the social forces against which he most polemicized; and from Samuel Johnson to F.R. Leavis he has been denounced in his turn, as a poet with a political chip on his shoulder or a perverse tormentor of the language of the nation.

Catherine Belsey's lucid study launches a subtle double reading of Milton's work, attending at once to its most negative ideological features and to those troubled 'textual' moments when his poems significantly equivocate, running against the grain of their official convictions. The act of poetry for Milton affirms a unity of time and eternity, past and present, the Logos and the human word; but this vision is inevitably submitted to the pluralizing, differentiating movement of writing, striving as it does to incarnate a Meaning of meanings which must remain elusive. Belsey finds in the poetry a play of contending voices and positions, never quite containable by its 'monological' control; and nothing could be more striking in this respect than the dense, burnished idiom of *Paradise Lost*, which foregrounds its own materiality in the very act of mediating a world beyond time.

Milton's oppressive patriarchalism is here registered in full, but also that which gives it the slip: the central eloquence of the lady of *Comus*, the failure of *Paradise Lost* to 'fix the meaning of sexual difference'. Milton is read as a 'humanist', trusting to a sovereign essence of Man; yet there are those forces within the poems which bring their authority to hesitate and come momentarily unstuck, a desire and difference which refuse to be wholly eradicated. Catherine Belsey's book will give little comfort to those for whom Milton stands in the pantheon of Great Englishmen; but it suggests, forcefully and intricately, ways in which his works might become freshly available today.

Terry Eagleton

Acknowledgements

I am grateful to Toril Moi and her colleagues at the Centre for Feminist Research in Bergen for a most productive seminar on *Comus*. And I am conscious of what I owe to Art Frank, who has written the best book ever on Lacan, and to Balachandra Rajan, subtlest of Milton's readers. Other debts – to James Dale, Liz and Norman Feltes, Laurence Green, Linda Hutcheon and Chris Weedon – are more subliminal, or more diffuse, but no less real for that. My graduate class at McMaster University in 1986 didn't mention Milton, but they were a pure delight. Sean Hand gave me a useful reference. Donald Hill authorized Daphne. Philip Carpenter is the most patient person I know. Antony Easthope, Peter W. Thomas and Terry Eagleton read the typescript, and the book is better for their acute and helpful comments. And indispensably, Andrew Belsey nourished and sustained the whole venture.

Acknowledgements

1   Turning-points

1.1 Incarnation

An undifferentiated peace prevails on earth. No sound of conflict disturbs the silence. The winds subside and the stars stand
still. Power is suspended. All at once an unearthly music is
heard, and radiant light dispels the darkness. The world is
irreversibly transformed.

Words on a page, verse, a gift to the infant God.

Milton's poetry records a series of moments when, at either
the local or the cosmic level, the relations between heaven and
earth are decisively changed. 'The Morning of Christ's Nativity' is such a moment.[1] The 'Ode' (1629) proclaims a descent
from heaven to earth, freely undertaken, when pure light for-
sakes its element for 'a darksome house of mortal clay' (line 14).
Peace too descends, traversing the celestial spaces, 'softly slid-
ing/Down through the turning sphere' (lines 47–8), with Truth
and Justice, and with Mercy, who sweeps through the clouds
from the courts of light. These concomitant descents, in conjunction with the Atonement as the purpose of the Incarnation,
bring about a new order and a new harmony between heaven
and earth, which is not yet complete, but which begins from this
instant. The dragon of sin is held from now on within narrower
confines, and the old gods are driven out, forsaking their tem-
ples as their falsehood is exposed. 'On the Morning of Christ's
Nativity' ('The Nativity Ode') thus represents the events which
constitute our 'redemption from above' (line 4).

It also offers to re-present redemption itself, to make it

present, inviting the reader to witness the Incarnation from a position where his or her individual and present redemption is both possible and imperative.

The poem evokes the familiar Nativity scene:

> It was the winter wild,
> While the heaven-born child
>   All meanly wrapped in the rude manger lies.
>   (29–31)

The 'star-led wizards' are there, hastening towards the stable (line 23), and the shepherds sit 'chatting' (line 87), with no thought of the mystery which is soon to confront them. At the end the text returns to the image of the Virgin and Child, and to the setting, now transformed to a 'courtly stable' filled with 'bright-harnessed' angels (lines 243–4), as majesty fuses with humility and light irradiates the darkness. But the implications of these events also ripple outwards to transform the condition of earth and ocean, and beyond them the cosmos. The conventional snow becomes an innocent covering for the guilty earth; winds and waters sink to rest. The stars are transfixed with awe, while the sun hides its light, eclipsed by a greater sun/Son. As heaven descends to earth, so earth goes down to hell when the old gods flock to their infernal prison.

Meanwhile, all time is simultaneously present and yet centred on the single moment of the Nativity. The music which greets the shepherds is also the song of the Sons of the Morning celebrating the creation of the world. The song is able to make time run back to the golden age, which is also, it seems, to make it run forward to the Second Coming, when Truth and Justice will appear in glory, throned on a rainbow, and the gates of heaven will be flung wide open. But then the text returns sharply to the present tense and to the moment in the stable:

> This must not yet be so,
>   The babe lies yet in smiling infancy.
>   (150–1)

What must be, however, in contrast to the joy of the present, is the future pain of the Atonement:

> The babe lies yet in smiling infancy
> That on the bitter cross
> Must redeem our loss.
>
> (151–3)

The Crucifixion in turn is the prelude the the Last Judgment, and only after that is the process of redemption complete:

> And then at last our bliss
> Full and perfect is,
>   But now begins.
>
> (165–7)

'But now begins.' What is the moment of this 'now'? There is none, or rather there are two, as the title of the poem implies and the Christian calendar permits. The morning of Christ's Nativity is a single historical occasion annually re-enacted, and in this sense the bliss that begins 'now', which is the bliss of redemption, begins both once and repeatedly. The tenses of the poem sustain that duality throughout: 'This *is* the month, and this the happy morn' when the Son of God 'Our great redemption from above *did* bring' (lines 1, 4) (my italics). The Incarnation is defined in the past tense, but the hymn, which is to be the baby's first gift, must reach him before the kings do, in the future. Thereafter the tenses defining the Nativity scene oscillate between past and present, but as the meaning of the Incarnation becomes increasingly apparent, the present begins to predominate. The pagan gods depart in the present, and the final vision of the stable invites the reader to 'see' the scene. The reference to the song itself, which is at once composed this Christmas and offered as a gift in the stable, has the effect of effacing the difference between this morning and that, the present from which that moment becomes the past:

> But see the virgin blest
> Hath laid her babe to rest.
>   Time is our tedious song should here have ending.
>
> (237–9)

In consequence of this superimposition, by which a single historical moment, in one sense irretrievably lost, is none the less recovered for 'now', the reader is made a witness in the present to the specific event and its temporal and cosmic implications.

It is the song of the angels, beyond all mortal music, divine, which effects the new-found harmony between heaven and earth, and which has the power to bring back the age of gold. This song is 'unexpressive' (line 116): inexpressible, perhaps, as all modern editors seem to insist, but also not expressive, not, that is, a sign of a presence which is elsewhere. The concord of the angels is not a substitute, an expression, existing in a relation of exteriority to the compact between the two realms. On the contrary, it is the bond itself: 'such harmony alone/Could hold all heaven and earth in happier union' (lines 107–8). Meanwhile, the old gods, their incantations silenced, find a new discordant music in moaning and lamentation, the cymbals of Moloch and the lowing of Osiris the bull, 'timbrelled anthems dark' (line 219), 'A drear and dying sound' (line 193).

What, then, in this context, is the status of the 'Ode' itself as song? The text offers a surprising answer:

> See how from far upon the eastern road
> The star-led wizards haste with odours sweet,
> O run, prevent them with thy humble ode,
> And lay it lowly at his blessed feet;
> Have thou the honour first thy Lord to greet,
>   And join thy voice unto the angel quire,
> From out his secret altar touched with hallowed fire.
>
> (22–8)

The 'Ode' is to be part of the angelic consort, a voice in that divine polyphony which is the bond between God and human beings, the union of heaven and earth. And the text makes this confident assertion on the grounds that the poem itself is the utterance of lips touched with fire from the altar of God:

> Then flew one of the Seraphims unto me, having a live coal in his hand, which he had taken with the tongs from off the altar: And he laid it upon my mouth, and said, Lo, this hath touched thy lips; and thine iniquity is taken away, and thy sin purged. Also I heard the voice of the Lord, saying, Whom shall I send, and who will go for us? Then said I, Here am I; send me. (Isaiah vi, 6–8)

The allusion of line 28 of the 'Ode' is to a descent from heaven which is both itself redemptive and a prelude to the prophecy of redemption. In the following chapter the newly authorized Isaiah was to prophesy the Incarnation: 'Behold, a virgin shall conceive, and bear a son, and shall call his name Immanuel' (Isaiah vii, 14). 'And they shall call his name Emmanuel, which being interpreted is, God with us' (Matthew i, 23). The promise, authorized from God's own altar, is 'God with us', a compact between God and human beings, a union of heaven and earth.

The 'Ode' claims prophetic status, and like the Old Testament prophets it too promises redemption. The prophets speak with the voice of God. The gift of the 'Ode' to the infant God is thus at the same time a gift of redemption to the human reader, a redemption of which God himself is in every sense the author. Like the Incarnation itself, the text is to make present the divinity of Christ, the Word of God incarnate in words. A promise, a performative, not the expression of a meaning which is elsewhere, not a sign of harmony, but the unexpressive bond itself, a part of the angelic song, the 'Ode' is offered as a redemptive text.

It is an ambitious claim, and the mode of the poem is no less ambitious. 'On the Morning of Christ's Nativity' was written when John Milton was twenty-one. The song which heralded the Nativity, and which demonstrated the presence of the divine in the human world, evidently also announced the birth of a poet.

1.2 The project

This book is not about John Milton. Readers anxious to treat Milton's writing as a means of access to something beyond itself, the 'mind' of a long-dead individual, may prefer to consult a critical biography of the author.[2] Here 'Milton' marks a moment in English textual history, and this book is about that moment in its history and its textuality.

I do not mean to suggest, of course, that John Milton did not exist as an individual, that he did not write Milton's texts, or that this process of production was in any way negligible. But I want to resist the conventional critical assumption that Milton himself is available, ready to be invoked as the ultimate

explanation of his writing. My reading of his texts is not necessarily one that John Milton would have recognized or acknowledged. Interpretation is not – cannot be – an activity of
reconstructing an intended meaning which preceded the writing
process. This traditional quarry of criticism is always a phantom
– not merely elusive and probably illusory, but also dead. The
author's intended meaning died in the moment that the text
came into being, and the text is necessarily more than the author
conceived or knew. The interpretation I want to offer does not
seek out an apparition; instead it attends to an appearance, the
signifying surface of the text, not an essence concealed by the
words, but the textuality of the words themselves.

Words are not entirely under our control. Neither authors nor
readers give them their meanings. On the contrary, it is the
process of learning their meanings which releases the possibility
of writing or reading, meaning or understanding. And meaning, in turn, is an effect of difference, finding its cause not in a
prior substance or a concept, but in a relationship which is also
an absence, the spacing between one signifier and another.

In Jacques Derrida's analysis the difference which makes
meaning possible is linked in the term 'differance' with the
deferment of what is meant.[3] Meaning is not only what is differed, differentiated, but also what is deflected by the signifier,
and in that sense what is always and inevitably absent. Writing,
then, is a process of substitution which is also one of relegation.
In a double and antithetical movement it both conjures up
meaning and supplants it. Reading in its conventional understanding and practice has been deeply imbued with a metaphysical desire for meaning as presence, for access to the
relegated, supplanted 'thought', intention or idea, which common sense so often locates 'behind' the text itself. But the spatial
metaphor betrays the impossibility of the project: the meaning is
elsewhere and is thus inaccessible. Only the signifier is within
reach.

Reading can therefore be no more than attention to the
signifier. This does not imply that we cannot talk about mean-
ing(s). The claim that the *opposition* between signifier and
signified is metaphysical does not eliminate the *difference* between
them.[4] Signifiers do signify, do differentiate. But because the
signifier cannot be anchored to a fixed, anterior presence

'behind' it, meaning is always unstable, plural, dispersed and disseminated.

Nor does the proposition that reading attends to the signifier imply that meaning is no longer an issue, that criticism concentrates on 'form' as distinct from 'content'. That distinction is itself metaphysical, reaffirming the notion that form is a kind of decorative but translucent container for an idea, an intention, an intelligibility, which could equally exist in some other form, or independently. Pure meaning does not exist on its own, independent of the signifier. But although meaning, absolute and unconditional, does not exist, it does not follow that nothing means anything. On the contrary, precisely on account of difference, meanings do exist – in their materiality and their effectivity. They are, however, an effect of interpretation, not its origin.

An interpretation is also a text. It is not a replica of the first text (Milton's). Nor is it a transcription of the phantom intention. It is not, in fact, a transcription of anything outside language, but a set of signifiers concerning another set of signifiers. There are cases where drawings, or gestures or music have been offered as interpretations of written texts, but these too are signifying practices. There is no interpretation and no understanding outside signifying practice.

My interpretation of Milton's plural, disseminated texts lays claim, then, to no special authority. I have no access to the meaning, absolute and unconditional, of these writings or any others. Does it follow that anything goes, that any interpretation is as good as any other, that 'it's all subjective', as they say?

Not at all. Meaning is no more located in the subjectivity of the reader than in the mind of the writer. The identification of meaning as subjective reaffirms the metaphysical notion of pure intelligibility independent of the signifier, meaning as an idea which precedes the signifying difference. Meaning in its plurality and its dissemination is public, linguistic and conventional: what it is possible for those (differential) signifiers to mean or to have meant.

But since the plurality remains, why this interpretation rather than any other? There are already plenty of readings of Milton around. And why Milton? There are in my view two answers to the latter question. The first is worth a paragraph and the second will take the rest of this book. There are two answers because the question is (of course) plural. In so far as it asks why *Milton's* texts, why this grouping of texts marked by the name of the author, my answer is that the English examination syllabus still all too frequently arranges the material for study under authors' names, at least to the extent that it continues to share the nineteenth-century assumption that the works signed by an author must in some continuous way express, and so make present, not only the phantom intention which lies behind the text, but the even more spectral subjectivity which is its origin. Students are still required to write essays about authors. And one way of trying to intervene in this state of affairs is to start from where things are. For that reason, too, I shall tend to concentrate on the familiar texts.

But in so far as the question asks why *Lycidas*, or *Samson Agonistes*, or *Paradise Lost*, my answer is more complex. These texts, readily available in modern editions, are part of a continuing history. They chart, I shall argue, some of the struggles and transformations which brought into being the world we now inhabit. They also constitute an intervention in those struggles and transformations. They record and participate in the historical turning-point which marks the installation of the modern epoch.

There is a close relationship between power and meaning. Despotic regimes have always attempted to take control of meaning, to fix it in their own interests, outlawing alternatives by making them literally unthinkable. In democratic societies the contest for meaning is also a struggle for power. If it were possible to pin down the single, authorized, guaranteed meaning of, say, masculine and feminine, or literature, freedom, or democracy itself, it would in consequence be possible to delimit those categories, excluding or repudiating as inadmissible whatever did not fit the definition. Social institutions reproduce and extend their own power by arresting the inevitable play of meaning.

In the Middle Ages it was probably the Catholic Church that made the most unremitting efforts to take institutional control of meaning. While God held in place the real meaning of good and truth, evil and heresy were excommunicated, burned and relegated to hell. It is not surprising, therefore, that in the cause of advancing the interests of the English nation-state and the absolute power of the Tudor monarchy, Henry VIII declared himself head of the Church of England. Evidently it was imperative to lay claim to the Church's power of determining meaning and truth. But the unforeseen price of Reformation was also the decentring of the Church as an institution. Protestant truth found its differentiating, defining others not only in popery, but also in the array of separatist sects, which challenged the power of the sovereign over their consciences, their religious and social practices and ultimately, if they still refused to conform, their bodies. The 'resolution' of these conflicts was also the founding moment of the modern world.

The sects reread the Scriptures and proclaimed themselves the true interpreters of the sacred text. In the twentieth century the institution of English, far less powerful than the medieval Church, but by no means negligible in its influence, assumes command of meaning in the compulsory school discipline of English language, and struggles to control of the range of admissible readings of texts through the apparatus of literary criticism. It fails, of course. In the event Milton has been read for and against theocentrism, for and against humanism, for and against sexism. The project in many of these instances has been to enlist the author, a great writer, a genius, Milton, in support of a cause. Alternatively, and notoriously in Milton's case, the poet is condemned for his bad verses, which means that there is no need to pay any attention to his radical political views.

Thus interpretation, like writing itself, constitutes an affirmation of values, an intervention in the struggle for meaning. My own interpretation is no exception. But I shall be less concerned that most earlier critics with Milton's genius (or lack of it), the unity of his texts (for better or worse), and the singularity of his wisdom (or wickedness). On the contrary, my interest is precisely in the plurality of the texts and the contests for meaning played out within them. Milton's writings, as I read them, demonstrate the conflicts between heaven and earth, authority and freedom, man and woman, which were ostensibly resolved in the creation of the modern world. In the twentieth century it is no longer obvious that all those conflicts were resolved to our satisfaction. In addition, the texts display a struggle to master meaning itself, and their failure demonstrates the triumph of language in its creativity. All these issues, identifiable in Milton's writing, are perhaps in a special way issues for us now. For that reason the texts seem to me worth rereading.

1.3 History

The period of Milton's writing, from the 1620s to 1674, was a turning-point in English history. Conflicts of interest in the economy and elsewhere, which had been building up for decades, often in excess or even in spite of the conscious intentions of their protagonists, came to a head in the Revolution of the 1640s, and though much that was radical in that war was lost in the hesitations of the interregnum and the reaction of the Restoration, the transformation that had taken place proved in the event to have been irrevocable. Change was confirmed and substantiated in 1688, with the effect that the world of the late seventeenth century was in many ways recognizably modern.[5]

The economy had been subject to gradual change since the early years of the sixteenth century. The Tudor construction of a strong, centralized nation-state provided the stability and the communications necessary for the expansion of commerce beyond the immediate locality. At the same time, the sale in the course of the century of former monastic and crown property released farmland on to the commercial market, and the rises in food prices as a result of inflation ensured that agricultural land was an investment. Opportunities for overseas trade increased with the creation by royal charter of a series of trading companies in the second half of the sixteenth century. These changes were in themselves the source of considerable social mobility, but they also brought with them an enhanced demand for professional services. The Church and the education system both provided increasing employment in the sixteenth and seventeenth centuries, and the legal profession offered the chance to make considerable fortunes as the law was adjusted to serve the interests of an emerging bourgeoisie.

The aspirations of the Tudor and Stuart monarchs were to varying degrees absolutist. Parliament, which was responsible for taxation and thus for a substantial element of the royal revenue, prevented these aspirations from being realized. But Parliament was not inevitably a source of resistance to the monarchy. The Commons was elected by and represented the emerging class of small property owners whose prosperity was an effect of the new regime. The gentry also supplied the officers of the militia, and kept order in the country as Justices of the Peace. JPs were appointed by the Crown. There was thus a certain community of interests between the monarchy and the House of Commons.

There was at the same time, however, a conflict between absolutist control of the economy and the emergence of a free market. Government policy throughout the period tended to restrict in various ways the development of the forces of production, and if the policy largely failed, this was only because the system of regulation was not effective. The conflict had implications for the relations between Crown and Parliament, which degenerated sharply in the reign of Charles I. As a result, the King insisted on his right to rule without parliamentary impediment. From 1629 to 1640 there were no Parliaments, and there was in consequence a serious problem of revenue. The conspicuous extravagance, which operated as a signifier precisely of Charles's right to do without Parliament, inevitably incurred considerable expense, and some of the expedients employed to raise money during the period made the existing conflict of interests inescapably visible. Landowners were fined for encroaching on obsolete medieval boundaries; monopolies were created purely in order to be sold, putting existing manufacturers out of business. Ultimately absolutism was incompatible with enterprise, competition and the freedom of trade.

The government's right to grant monopolies was abolished in 1641; it was not revived at the Restoration. Feudal tenures and the Court of Wards were abolished in 1646, and this was confirmed in 1660. Thereafter the Privy Council made no further attempt to impose taxes without parliamentary consent. The House of Lords, abolished in 1649, was restored, but during the reign of Charles II the Commons established the right to initiate money bills which were not subject to amendment by the Lords. The prerogative courts were not revived, and patronage devolved increasingly on to ministers.

While the Commons moved resolutely towards taking control

of the government of the realm on behalf of property owners, there emerged from the mid-seventeenth century onwards institutional support for the development of an economy based on the circulation of commodities. In London banks permitted deposits which were subject to withdrawal or transfer by means of cheques. Short-term credit, as well as the transmission of money without the danger and difficulty of moving large quantities of coin, were thus readily and consistently available in the capital. After 1640 mortgages became common as a means of raising money. Fire insurance developed in London as a result of the devastation of property by the Great Fire of 1666. Trunk roads improved from the 1660s onwards, and the Post Office emerged as an indispensable service. These changes were accompanied by an increase in the number of joint-stock companies, the growth of factories, and a dramatic increase in consumption. Derek Hirst, who has little sympathy with the analysis of the period as revolutionary, nevertheless draws attention to the emergence in the seventeenth century of the consumer society, especially in the sphere of household goods, textiles and fashion. And he adds, 'by the 1650s a major landmark was visible with the appearance of coffee shops in London and Oxford'.[6]

The poor on the whole got poorer in consequence, and the bourgeoisie became richer, more secular, and less deferential. The new ruling class asserted its authority most obviously not only by ruthlessly buying and discarding labour-power, but also by rendering domestic servants largely invisible for the first time. In the Elizabethan period 'the family' included the servants, which does not, of course, imply that they were not exploited, but only that they were expected to be in evidence. During the second half of the seventeenth century, domestic architecture began to take account of the emerging distinction between public and private. The new nuclear family dined together in the dining room, while the servants tended to be relegated to the kitchen or the servants' hall. The development of corridors and back stairs also helped to foster privacy, as well as keeping the servants out of sight. It was at this stage, too, that male servants began to be replaced by women, who were cheaper to hire.[7]

Nature, too, was to be mastered. The Royal Society of the

1660s continued the discussions which had begun in Oxford a decade earlier, with particular emphasis on experimental science. The Society in its early years helped to stimulate developments in agriculture, navigation and the manufacture of precision instruments. There were advances in chemistry, botany, medicine, mathematics and astronomy. The aim was to subject nature to the knowing gaze and the improving labour of the human scientist.

In addition, the Royal Society contributed to the encouragement of the plain style. Language in its wayward textuality was also to be brought under control. Proposals for an academy to reform and stabilize English came in the end to nothing, but the empiricist view triumphed in language as in science. The virtues of the best writing were now clarity, plainness and transparency, to the point where even metaphor was suspected of betraying the simplicity and the singularity of the signified. Language became at this moment the instrument of a meaning which was located elsewhere, in the consciousness of the knowing, controlling individual, the humanist subject. Humanism, which had gradually defined its terms in the course of two centuries, was now sure enough of its own dominance to regard its main propositions as free-standing, independent of the signifier, literally self-evident.

The English Revolution, then, changed the world. This apparently ethnocentric claim is deliberate: the imperialism which accompanied the installation of capitalism eventually transformed the relations between Europe and all the other continents. Milton himself was deeply immersed in the revolutionary process – as its apologist and theorist, its conscience and, on occasions, its castigator. His prose writings of the 1640s and 50s include instances of political persuasion and political denunciation which remain unsurpassed. Early in the revolutionary period Milton was regarded as dangerously radical. Though he did not share the communism of the Diggers and some of the Ranters, he was deeply opposed to privilege, impatient with social institutions and passionately committed to individual liberty – at least for the faithful, God's elect. Later, as some of the optimism of the early days began to evaporate, his commitment to private property and social hierarchy became more apparent. This was, after all, a revolution which had the effect of establishing the bourgeoisie as the ruling class.

This book is not primarily about Milton's contributions to the specific political debates of his time. Christopher Hill's *Milton and the English Revolution* brilliantly and authoritatively analyses Milton's views, in the light of an unmatchable knowledge of seventeenth-century history.[8] (I might venture, though, to disagree with Hill's evaluation of Milton's humanism, or his sexual politics.) My project is not to identify Milton's beliefs but to locate in Milton's texts, sometimes in defiance of the author's apparent convictions, the turbulence within the writing which demonstrates the conflicts that occurred in the process of establishing some of the meanings we now take for granted. If Milton's writing displays one singular quality, it is a remorseless refusal to settle for easy solutions or shallow generalizations. When *Paradise Lost*, for instance, does not immediately resolve the problems of power it raises, it returns to the questions, reopens them in different terms, and tries again.

This issue of power, and the others I shall discuss, are issues specifically of the seventeenth century. The flight of (imaginary) presence from textuality and the emergence of language as the instrument of meaning took place in that period. Similarly, the construction of marriage as a realm of harmony, above and beyond the (legitimate) brutality of the market-place, was effected in the century which followed the Reformation, and cemented in the revolutionary decades. Sovereignty was transferred in this period from the monarch to those of 'the people' who were held to be authoritative because they possessed the truth (and a certain amount of property). These new values of the seventeenth century, which have become the great 'obviousnesses' of the modern world, were not established without a struggle, and Milton's texts make visible for us now the chasms which were precariously bridged and the fierce repression of alternatives which took place in the process.

Recent history has thrown some of these obviousnesses into question once again: the transparency of language, the sanctity of marriage and the sovereignty of truth have all been challenged in the twentieth century. In denaturalizing the meanings we have taken for granted, demonstrating that they were produced at a specific historical moment, and that they bear the marks of conflict in their instability, Milton's texts can be read as reaffirming these twentieth-century challenges, placing the modern reader in consequence as a participant in history and in struggle.

1.4 Authority

Like 'The Nativity Ode', *Paradise Lost* (1658–63?) records a turning-point in the relations between heaven and earth:

> Of man's first disobedience, and the fruit
> Of that forbidden tree, whose mortal taste
> Brought death into the world, and all our woe,
> With loss of Eden, till one greater man
> Restore us, and regain the blissful seat,
> Sing . . .

(Paradise Lost I, 1–6)

This time it is the Fall which is decisive, bringing in its wake new conditions of human existence, a destiny of death, woe and loss. The mortal taste of the fruit puts an end to human immortality: the similarities between human beings and the angels are sharply reduced, and as a result Adam and Eve are no longer entitled to inhabit a garden which is the earthly counterpart of heaven. The source of the tragedy is human disobedience to the divine authority. In consequence, while God remains in place, unchanged, human life is irrevocably transformed.

God's authority, like his fixity, is an absolute in *Paradise Lost*: it is nowhere questioned. And yet the protagonist of these opening lines – and, it might be argued, of the text as a whole – is 'man', who disobeys and tastes the fruit and brings death. Who, then, initiates and determines human history? God, who imposed the prohibition? Or 'man', who broke it? The setting of the story is not heaven but earth, the world; and the tragic consequence is *our* woe. Who, then, does the story belong to? God, as creator of the world? Or 'man', who inhabits it, for better or worse?[9]

The providential comedy which provides the structural framework of the narrative necessitates a second turning-point, a reversal of the Fall and the promise of redemption, through the intervention of 'one greater man'. The phrase is both inevitable and surprising: it is as man that Christ carries out the

Atonement, and as the second Adam that he reverses the implications of the Fall (Romans v, 11–19). At the same time, the
reiteration of the word 'man' in this synopsis of the poem's
theme has the effect of foregrounding the human identity of its
protagonists. If Providence directs events, it is 'man' who enacts
them, bringing divine comedy into conjunction with humanist
epic. The ambiguity of the Incarnation deepens the questions
already posed: who determines history? what are the limits of
the human? The stress on freedom of choice throughout the text,
and the final promise of a 'paradise within' as a state of human
consciousness (XII, line 587) leave the questions unresolved.

Many of Milton's poems record such turning-points, whether
cosmic or personal, and often they address in the process questions concerning the location of authority. If *Paradise Lost*
ponders the issue across twelve books, Sonnet XVI, 'On his
Blindness' (1652?) dramatizes it succinctly in fourteen lines.
The occasion of the poem is loss, not only of sight, but in consequence of 'that one talent which is death to hide' (line 3), the
power to serve God as his poet. Patience, who rebukes the
doubting, distrustful speaker, and urges submission, claims to
speak with the authority of God. What Patience says is certainly
right: God has things under control. That the poem exists as an
affirmation of God's unsearchable ways, in defiance of the
poet's despair, is itself the evidence which proves Patience's
case: clearly in practice the one talent is being fully employed.
And yet in the poem it is precisely the human doubt which
motivates the affirmation – and enlists the reader in the process
of catechism which prompts Patience's account of the divine
authority.

Lycidas (1637) confronts another turning-point. This poem is
a meditation on the implications of death. What is the meaning
of the divine promise, of the one talent, if death prevents its
realization? What are the obligations of the poet whose voice is
not heard? What are the limits of the power of human 'song'?
And if *Lycidas* records a death, *Samson Agonistes* (1647–53)[10]
might be read as an allegory of all our woe, a story of human
failure – and renewal. Because he has betrayed the secret of
the promise, Samson is helpless in the power of his enemies,
enslaved by the prince of this world. He confronts despair, and
recovers. It is time which restores his strength, and divine grace

which initiates the revival of his will to act: but it is Samson himself who exacts revenge.

Paradise Regained (1667–70?) shows the promise of redemption fulfilled. Christ's resistance to temptation is presented as the critical turning-point which reverses the implications of the Fall. In 'The Nativity Ode' redemption comes 'from above' (line 4); in *Paradise Regained*, forty years later, and twenty years after the Revolution, though the theology of the Incarnation has not changed, its presentation is radically different. In contrast to the 'Ode', *Paradise Regained* relegates its supernatural figures to the margins of the action; in contrast to *Paradise Lost*, it presents no cosmic wars. Instead 'one greater man' confronts a single adversary whose main weapon, despite his magic powers, is persuasive argument. Is the victory of the second Adam necessarily superhuman?

In other words, Milton's poems reproduce as questions some of the issues at the heart of the historical transformation they also help to bring about. All Milton's writing can be read as addressing, directly or indirectly, the question of the meaning of 'man'. *De doctrina Christiana* is his Latin prose summary of Christian doctrine, if summary is the proper word for a text of nearly 700 pages. Like *Paradise Lost*, with which it is probably roughly contemporary, the *Christian Doctrine* insists, against the prevailing current of Calvinist orthodoxy, on human freedom, though without in any way undermining or diminishing the divine authority (pp. 155–202).[11] More radically still, *Christian Doctrine* repudiates centuries of neo-Platonic Christian dualism, in favour of a neo-Aristotelean understanding of what it is to be a person. The soul is no longer an independent and immortal entity in conflict with the body. Instead, a human being is a single, unified individual (undivided):

> He is not double or separable: not, as is commonly thought, produced from and composed of two different and distinct elements, soul and body. On the contrary, the whole man is the soul, and the soul the man: a body, in other words, or individual substance, animated, sensitive, and rational.
>
> (p. 318)

If the vocabulary of this section of the text looks back to Aristotle, the proposition also points forward unequivocally to humanism.

The questions humanism raises recur throughout Milton's work: what are the limits of human autonomy and human obligation? what is the place of human beings in the world and in history? and what, beyond all history and all locality, does it mean to be human? The questions are not fully answered, cannot be fully answered in so far as they presuppose a Christian or a humanist metaphysics. But if the texts cannot make present for the reader a transcendent essence of the human, they nevertheless succeed in displaying how deeply the problems they pose are implicated in related questions concerning the specificities of gender, power and, above all, the textuality of meaning itself.

2 Poetry

2.1 Presence

The rich surface of 'On the Morning of Christ's Nativity' hides
no mysteries, veils no dim and undetermined sense of unknown
modes of being. Indeed, this is a text which conceals nothing,
least of all its own art. On the contrary, clearly defined
allegorical figures, glowing with light, steer purposefully
through the immensity of space; cherubim and seraphim 'Are
seen in glittering ranks with wings displayed' (line 114); even
the music of the spheres evokes awe without incomprehen-
sibility. Moreover, there is no real need to consult modern foot-
notes for details about the banished gods, Peor and Baalim,
Ashtaroth and Moloch: the recitation of their alien names places
paganism as other and relegates it in consequence to a world of
palpable evil. 'The Nativity Ode' is not in any sense reticent
about its meaning, which is there for all to see.

Nor is the poem concerned to offer access to an empirical
reality, the immediate particularity of the stable, the feelings of
the shepherds, or the sensations of motherhood. Like a baroque
painting, crowded with grand figures in swirling movement
round a still centre, the 'Ode' lays claim not to specificity but
to magnificence. Consequently, the text is not a transparent
medium through which we are invited to encounter an experience. Instead the poem offers to act, to bring the redemptive
meaning of the Incarnation before the reader. The project of
magnificence is to require obedience, submission, and the magnificence of the 'Ode' signifies its redeeming authority. The

meaning and implications of the Nativity are thus present in this seventeenth-century text, not elsewhere, behind or beyond it, where twentieth-century common sense colloquially places meaning. The reader has only to obey its imperative – 'But see . . . ' (line 237) in both senses – to participate individually in the universal redemption the text defines.

The still centre of the poem, the smiling child, is at the moment of the Incarnation both transcendental signified, the meaning which holds all other meanings in place (God), and absolute signifier, meaning undivided from itself (God made visible). Christ is the Logos, Word and concept held together. The location of the Word for Protestantism is the Bible, Word of God and thus redemptive text, but the Word is also affirmed in the word of the preacher who calls sinners to repentance. Poetry, Milton maintained in *The Reason of Church Government* (1642), is like preaching in its redemptive power. The Bible is full of poetry. The 'songs' of the Law and the Prophets are the result of poetic inspiration which, as the gift of God, may be found in all nations and at all times. Such songs 'are of power beside the office of a pulpit, to imbreed and cherish in a great people the seeds of virtue.' And Milton himself promises to contribute to this process with a work of prophetic significance, produced by inspiration, as a result of 'devout prayer to that eternal Spirit who can enrich all utterance and knowledge, and sends out his seraphim with the hallowed fire of his altar to touch and purify the lips of whom he pleases' (*The Reason of Church Government*, pp. 816, 820–1).[1]

The project of such poetry is to inscribe the Word in the word: not merely to represent meaning but to make it present, to realize presence in its plenitude and its magnificence. But there are problems. The prophetic voice is simultaneously divine and human. The moment of 'The Nativity Ode' is both in time and beyond its constraints. The presence the poem seeks to realize depends precisely on eliminating the differences of which it is composed. The result is a hesitation of the tenses, a reluctance to claim authority, which indicate that the project of the text, the inscription of the undifferentiated Word in a system of differences, defies the nature of language itself.

One of the triumphs of 'On the Morning of Christ's Nativity', I have suggested, is its superimposition of this Christmas on

that, so that they are one redemptive moment. But this triumph
is also an acknowledgement, as the tenses oscillate between past
and present, that Christmas is on the one hand a single event,
the Nativity, enacted and irrecoverable, and on the other its
celebration, re-enacted annually. The process of superimposition depends precisely on this difference. In the text the
meaning of the Incarnation is an effect of its place in the scheme
of redemption, especially its relationship to the Atonement. But
for a witness in the stable this meaning is not yet evident, not yet
established. It is important, therefore, not to efface the moment
of the poem, the present from which the past is retrospectively
intelligible and therefore redemptive. At the same time, it is
equally important to make present the originary event. But the
text can do this only, as the shifting tenses indicate, by ousting a
future to which, nevertheless, it constantly returns as its difference and its interpretation:

> This must not yet be so,
>   The babe lies yet in smiling infancy,
> That on the bitter cross
> Must redeem our loss;
>   So both himself and us to glorify.
>   (150–4)

'Our loss', 'us'. What exactly is the place of the poet/prophet
whose lips are touched and purified with the hallowed fire?
Who, in other words, is speaking? The introduction to the
Hymn suggests that it is the Muse of Christian poetry, divinely
authorized:

> Say heavenly Muse, shall not thy sacred vein
> Afford a present to the infant God?
> Hast thou no verse, no hymn, or solemn strain,
> To welcome him?
>   (15–18)

The prophetic allusion confirms this divine authority: the voice
of God speaks through his chosen poet and guarantees the truth
of the promise the text affirms (line 28). But the speaker whose
poem is a gift to God, a bond between heaven and earth, is
clearly not God but human – and subject to human limits.
What are we to make of the authority of a speaker who promises

redemption but who is uncertain whether the song of the angels is really the same as the creation hymn:

> Such music (as 'tis said)
> Before was never made,
>   But when of old the sons of morning sung.
>   (117–19)

What justifies the confidence of a human poet who has not heard for himself the music of the spheres?

> Ring out, ye crystal spheres,
> Once bless out human ears,
>   (If ye have power to touch our senses so).
>   (125–7)

This difference within the speaking voice of the text, these uncertainties and hesitations, come close momentarily to identifying the authority of the poem as imaginary, and its affirmation of presence as no more than a reaffirmation of an anterior textuality, what 'is said' by others, by other texts.

The 'Ode' as song is continuous with the music of the angels. In Milton's poetry, song, a combination of words and music, harmonious and 'unexpressive', is consistently a signifier of the fullness, the undifferentiated unity of presence realized. In 'At a Solemn Music' (1633?) voice and verse joined in song are defined as 'pledges of heaven's joy' (line 1). As 'pledges', they are both a promise of the future (heaven) and an event in the present (on earth), an enacting of the promise, its performative. There is thus a close parallel between this poem and the 'Ode'. The text incites the 'Solemn Music' itself to 'present' on earth the song which everlastingly surrounds the throne of God (line 5). This song is also

> the fair music that all creatures made
> To their great Lord, whose love their motion swayed
> In perfect diapason, whilst they stood
> In first obedience.
>
>   (21–4)

Whose is the 'love' of line 22? God's, whose love controlled the harmony, ruled it from above? Or the creatures', whose love of God determined their 'perfect diapason' (concord)? It does not matter, of course: the love is one and the same, the perfect union of heaven and earth in one undivided will before the Fall. And the appeal of the poem is for the recreation of that song in this,

> That we on earth with undiscording voice
> May rightly answer that melodious noise.
>
> (17–18)

And yet here too, and more emphatically than in 'The Nativity Ode', the difference between past and present disrupts the affirmation of the promise:

> That we on earth with undiscording voice
> May rightly answer that melodious noise;
> As once we did, till disproportioned sin
> Jarred against nature's chime, and with harsh din
> Broke the fair music that all creatures made.
>
> (17–21)

Is the lost harmony recoverable now in the pledge of performance, or is that only a 'phantasy' (line 5)? The poem seems unsure: 'O may we soon again renew that song,/And keep in tune with heaven' (lines 25–6).

The possibility of the inscription of the Word in the word, of the Logos in song, seems to recede into the future, a hope rather than a certainty. The fair music of harmony between heaven and earth can be named, but the mission of the poet requires that it be made audible.

2.2 Differance

Meaning is always an effect of difference between signifiers. And since meaning does not find its cause in a substance or a concept, but only in difference itself, there is also a difference within the signified, the trace of otherness within the self-same, a result of the inevitable allusion to difference itself, and so to the meanings that are excluded. But meaning is also a deferment, a distancing by the signifier, which is always a detour, of the concept or the substance it offers to represent. Signification suspends the referent; re-presentation separates the present or presence, however minutely, from itself. Derrida's term 'differance' points to both difference and deferment, and to their consequence. The signifier cannot make present, even in imagination, a single, full, masterable meaning-which-is-truth. It cannot incarnate the Logos. At the same time there is no meaning (and no Logos) outside signification. Differance 'maintains our relationship with that which we necessarily misconstrue, and which exceeds the alternative of presence and absence.'[2]

This melancholy recognition, or something like it, became available as the seventeenth-century Protestant church splintered into sects, each claiming access to salvation on the basis of the Word of God. With no single, central institution to guarantee the meaning of the Scriptures, authority was dispersed among a range of voices, each competing to promise redemption. But if the Word could not make present a single, masterable meaning-which-was-truth, that must be because the Logos had left the earth. The Fall, the moment of division between human and divine, therefore prised open in this period as never before the gap between signification and truth, earth and heaven.

This is the gap which begins to be glimpsed in 'The Nativity Ode' and is more clearly apparent in 'At a Solemn Music'. In each case the problem is evident in the question of voice. To lay claim to the truth is to speak with the voice of God from a position of divine omniscience. But to do so is to repudiate the human voice of the poet, and thus to widen the gap between heaven and earth, when the project is to close it by affirming redemption as a human reality. It is as a solution to this problem that 'sphere-borne' song can act as a pledge of heaven's joy in 'At a Solemn Music', but it is a consequence of it that 'we' cannot be certain of our ability to join in without discord.

In Dziga Vertov's film, *Man with a Movie Camera* (1928), the camera triumphantly swoops and glides from place to place, presenting the audience with long-shots and close-ups, showing familiar objects from unusual angles, and recording events which the human eye cannot possibly be in a position to see. The voice in 'The Nativity Ode' behaves in a rather similar way – and effects something like the same celebration of signifying power. The poet, who is not simply an omniscient third-person narrator, but speaks for 'us', does so from within the stable and from the cosmos, from the present and the past, laying claim to a knowledge of the future which implies divine authority, and acknowledging a human limitation on what can be known. But as I have suggested, it is exactly this triumphant versatility, this difference within the voice of the poet/prophet, that calls in question the authority of the text and begins the Fall into differance.

Milton's poetry continues to be haunted by the problem of voices which query presence even while they construct it. Sonnet XVI, 'On his Blindness' confronts the issue directly by isolating the doubting voice of the human speaker from the authoritative voice of virtue:

> When I consider how my light is spent,
>   Ere half my days, in this dark world and wide,
>   And that one talent which is death to hide,
>   Lodged with me useless, though my soul more bent
> To serve therewith my maker, and present
>   My true account, lest he returning chide,
>   Doth God exact day-labour, light denied,
>   I fondly ask. But Patience to prevent
> That murmur, soon replies, God doth not need
>   Either man's work or his own gifts. Who best
>   Bear his mild yoke, they serve him best. His state
> Is kingly: thousands at his bidding speed
>   And post o'er land and ocean without rest;
>   They also serve who only stand and wait.[3]

The two voices of the text are in marked contrast to each other. The first speaker, no longer the generalized 'we' of the earlier poems, is identified as a specific individual, a subjectivity struggling to make sense of the world amid a welter of subordinate clauses. Patience is authoritative, clear and paratactic. The Sonnet is thus dramatic as the previous texts are not. It solves the problem of voice in formal terms. We have no reason to doubt the authenticity of the 'I', who does no more than formulate a question (with whatever syntactic difficulty, and however 'fondly' – foolishly, as well as eagerly). But what guarantees the authority of Patience? Very little, except the syntax. The ringing main clauses in the second half of the Sonnet do not invite discussion or debate. Who would feel qualified to dispute the force of these emphatic assertions, culminating in a line which sounds like a piece of the proverbial wisdom (and has become so since)? Patience's position also has a broad scriptural authority, of course, though it quite alters the usual reading of the parable of the talents (Matthew xxv, 14–30). But 'On his Blindness' is a great deal more modest in its pretensions than 'The Nativity Ode', which claims the authority to make present the Logos. If the Sonnet offers meaning-which-is-truth, it does so as a matter of rhetoric, without anchoring the truth in any extra-textual source.

Comus (*A Masque Presented at Ludlow Castle*) (1634), is fully dramatic, and the problem of the authority of the speaker is here made explicit. The *Masque* displays an encounter between vice and virtue, rapacious enchanter and innocent lady. Comus employs the full resources of rhetoric to persuade the Lady to drink his magic potion, but she counters his 'wit' and 'dazzling fence' (lines 789–90) with a plain argument for temperance and an assertion of the value of chastity. Comus responds, but not to her words themselves:

> She fables not, I feel that I do fear
> Her words set off by some superior power;
> And though not mortal, yet a cold shuddering dew
> Dips me all o'er, as when the wrath of Jove
> Speaks thunder.

> (799–803)

The presence, the superior power which guarantees the truth of the Lady's words, is elsewhere. The text no longer fully trusts to the effectiveness of its own signifying processes. Nor does it trust its audience to distinguish rhetoric from truth, but feels it necessary to authorize in this way one of the conflicting voices. The villain explicitly concedes the case. In practice the precaution turns out to have been more than justified: despite Comus's response, a number of twentieth-century critics have still preferred to be convinced by the sensuous particularity of his earlier speeches, and to repudiate the egalitarian politics of the Lady's.[4] But the inclusion in the text of Comus's comment ironically acknowledges what criticism has so amply demonstrated, that truth cannot be sealed finally and incontrovertibly into words, and that interpretation always takes place from a position, on the basis of existing assumptions, presuppositions and values.

In hell the fallen angels seek solace and distraction in a number of pursuits. Some find it in 'song', singing to the accompaniment of the harp the story of their own heroic deeds and their tragic fall.

Their song was partial, but the harmony
(What could it less when spirits immortal sing?)
Suspended hell, and took with ravishment
The thronging audience.
(Paradise Lost II, 552–5)

The song is 'partial' (polyphonic as well as biased), but it has a magic power to distance hell. Others among the fallen angels take comfort in philosophy, a still more pleasing pastime, 'For eloquence the soul, song charms the sense' (line 556). The philosophy, of course, is false, 'Yet with a pleasing sorcery could charm/Pain for a while' (lines 566–7). The imagery (sorcery, charms) is of enchantment. Are song and eloquence therefore suspect? Or are *this* song and *this* eloquence magic only because they are false? The generalized nature of the comment suggests not: 'For eloquence the soul, song charms the sense'. But it implies a hierarchy in which eloquence (intellectual debate, philosophy) appeals to the higher faculty.

Comus the enchanter uses charms to ensnare the Lady (lines 757, 852), and she succumbs, at least to the extent that she follows him to his palace. The charms he displays for the audience are most evidently the 'Shakespearean' imagery of his rhetoric ('millions of spinning worms,/That in their green shops weave the smooth-haired silk' (lines 714–15).[5] But the suspicion that charms are confined to evil enchanters, and indeed the implication of the quotation from *Paradise Lost* that poetry is inferior to philosophy, are both dispelled in *Comus* in an engaging moment of recognition by the Second Brother (played by Thomas Egerton, aged nine). The Elder Brother describes the sun-clad power of chastity in verse which is marginally less Shakespearean than Comus's, but still gratifyingly full of ghosts and goblins, charnels and perilous wilds. The younger boy exclaims,

How charming is divine philosophy!
Not harsh, and crabbed as dull fools suppose,
But musical as is Apollo's lute,
And a perpetual feast of nectared sweets.

(475-8)

The enchantment is there and the sensual delight too, in an instance of authorized 'eloquence' which is both poetry and philosophy. The power of 'song' is reaffirmed.

But if the 'charm' of song is at once the property of hell, of wicked enchanters and of divine philosophy alike, how can the reader or the audience be sure to distinguish one from the other? How is delusion to be avoided? How can a poet be certain 'to imbreed and cherish . . . the seeds of virtue'?

Comus attempts to solve the problem by authorizing one of its voices. In *Lycidas* the problem of voice becomes critical; and so does the problem of poetry. The claims made in *Lycidas* on behalf of poetry are as high as ever. The whole text centres on the question of song. In accordance with the pastoral mode of the poem, the dead Lycidas was a shepherd. Shepherds conventionally sing (and play their oaten reeds). The text itself will be a song for a poet:

Who would not sing for Lycidas? he knew
Himself to sing, and build the lofty rhyme.

(10-11)

But it is also to be the song of a shepherd–poet: 'For we were nursed upon the self-same hill,/Fed the same flock' (lines 23-4). Thus the shepherd–speaker too may merit an elegy in due course (19-22).

The delicacy of the imagery should not be allowed to obscure the seriousness of the project. In a section which startlingly discards all delicacy the poem denounces bad shepherds and their 'lean and flashy songs' (line 123), which are no more than 'wind' and 'rank mist' (line 126). The passage differentiates those songs from this, the text itself, and in doing so offers to specify the limits beyond which poetry no longer cherishes virtue.

When *Lycidas* was printed for the second time in 1645, Milton included a headnote explaining that the poem 'by occasion foretells the ruin of our corrupted clergy then in their height'. This may have been a politic move in 1645, but it has tended to cloud for subsequent criticism the continuity and the complexity of the shepherd imagery which runs all the way through the text. In 1637, when the poem first appeared without the headnote, it would have been more readily apparent that the bad shepherds were bad poets as well as bad clergy. Throughout Milton's writing there is a parallel between the two. Poetry works 'beside the office of a pulpit' to cherish virtue. The prophetic character of the poet and the poetic quality of the Scriptures hold the link in place. The bad shepherds of *Lycidas* betray the sheep. They are

> Blind mouths! that scarce themselves know how to hold
> A sheep-hook, or have learned aught else the least
> That to the faithful herdman's art belongs!
>
> (119–21)

Their 'lean and flashy songs' are an echo of the 'new-fangled toys and trimming slight' characteristic of fashionable verse in 'At a Vacation Exercise' (1628), and perhaps too of Comus's 'dear wit, and gay rhetoric' (*Comus*, line 789).

Edward King, the Lycidas of the poem, as a Fellow of Christ's College, Cambridge, was in holy orders. He was also a poet. And the unnamed Shepherd who authorizes both vocations, origin and guarantee of the utterances of all good shepherds, is of course Christ himself.

But although in *Lycidas* poetry has lost none of its importance and has surrendered none of its high claims, and although the delusive charms of bad poetry are denounced more vehemently than ever before, the poem seems nevertheless to betray an uncertainty about the power of poetry which is not finally resolved. This hesitation begins with an allusion to Calliope, the muse of epic and the mother of a poet:

> What could the muse herself that Orpheus bore,
> The muse herself for her enchanting son
> Whom universal nature did lament,
> When by the rout that made the hideous roar,
> His gory visage down the stream was sent?
>
> (58–62)

In classical legend the song of Orpheus had the power to charm beasts and plants. In the moralized version of the story, common from the Middle Ages onwards, a parallel was drawn between Orpheus and the biblical poet, author of the Psalms, whose music was able to comfort the melancholy King Saul. In the humanist interpretation of the legend, which begins to appear in the sixteenth century, the music of Orpheus is able to control wild things because it is in tune with the universal harmony, the music of the spheres.[6] According to *Lycidas*, 'enchanting' Orpheus was torn to pieces by disordered and frenzied creatures whose own wild utterance was a 'hideous roar'. The muse could not save him.

Is it possible that bad poetry drives out good? Or that meaningless noise drives out poetry altogether? If so, is the herdman's art worth learning? At once the poem continues,

> Alas! What boots it with uncessant care
> To tend the homely slighted shepherd's trade,
> And strictly meditate the thankless muse?
>
> (64–6)

If fame is the motive, the speaker goes on, the death of Lycidas (and Orpheus, of course) demonstrates that a poet might not live to enjoy it. But Apollo, himself a poet, intervenes: 'Fame is no plant that grows on mortal soil' (line 78). Fame belongs in heaven, where 'all-judging Jove' makes the final assessment of poetic merit (line 82).

The crisis is averted and the conclusion of the poem anticipated: good poetry is recognized in heaven, if not on earth; Lycidas is in heaven, where he hears the saints, 'That sing, and singing in their glory move' (line 180). But it is striking that in this text God has become the *judge* of true poetry. He is no longer its author, as he was in 'The Nativity Ode'.

After the denunciation of the bad poets there follows, as if to demonstrate what can and should be done, a passage of perfect pastoral delicacy. Primroses and violets, cowslips and daffodils are summoned to strew the 'laureate' hearse of Lycidas (laurelled – for a poet). The surprise of what follows calls into question the confidence of the demonstration:

For so to interpose a little ease,
Let our frail thoughts dally with false surmise.
                    (152-3)

Lycidas has no hearse: he was drowned and the body was not
recovered. The flower passage is a cheat, escapism, its charms
pure wind and mist, frail thoughts dallying with a false surmise.

Nevertheless, Lycidas is now in heaven, where he hears 'the
unexpressive nuptial song' which surrounds the throne of God
(line 176). 'Unexpressive' is familiar from 'The Nativity Ode',
where it characterizes the song of the angels both as inexpressible and also as an instance of full presence, not an expression
of something else, but the thing itself, 'unexpressive' in that it
obliterates the differance of representation. In the 'Ode', however, the angels' song constitutes the bond between heaven and
earth, and signifies the miracle of redemption. By contrast, in
the economy of the later text it belongs in heaven, audible there
only. Presence has left the earth. There remains in this world
only a textuality from which the certainty of truth has fled,
enchantment which may prove to be a 'false surmise'.

The prophetic utterance is single and single-minded,
monologic, guaranteed as it is by the Word whose word it represents. *Lycidas* is composed of a range of voices. As in 'On his
Blindness', one of these is a questioning, doubting subject-
speaker. Antony Easthope has argued persuasively that the
iambic pentameter became the dominant mode of English verse
from the sixteenth century onwards, as the project of poetry was
increasingly to simulate the individual speaking voice. The
effect is a verse form which helps to construct the illusion of an
identifiable individual spontaneously expressing his or her subjective experience.[7] In a discussion specifically of 'On his Blindness', Easthope also points to the way that in this poem the
syntax rides across the rhyme scheme:

And that one talent which is death to hide,
Lodged with me useless, though my soul more bent
To serve therewith my maker, and present
My true account . . .
                    (3-6)

The effect, Easthope argues, is relatively to efface the signifier,
the materiality of the verse itself, metre, rhyme and rhythm, in

favour of the construction of an individual voice speaking, struggling, feeling.[8]

A similar strategy is developed in a slightly different way in *Lycidas*. Here the verse form is a freer version of the *canzone*, a mode considerably adapted and modified in sixteenth-century Italy. The *canzone* consists of a repeated long stanza with a complex rhyme scheme, and a shorter concluding stanza. The further modification of this form in *Lycidas* develops a tendency to counterpoint between rhyme scheme and sentence structure, so that the syntactic pauses frequently do not coincide with the ends of the couplets. In other words, where the rhyme points to closure, the syntax does not, except at the end of each verse paragraph. The resulting impression is of an intensity of feeling which is barely contained.[9]

> I come to pluck your berries harsh and crude,
> And with forced fingers rude,
> Shatter your leaves before the mellowing year.
> Bitter constraint, and sad occasion dear,
> Compels me to disturb your season due:
> For Lycidas is dead, dead ere his prime,
> Young Lycidas, and hath not left his peer:
> Who would not sing for Lycidas? he knew
> Himself to sing, and build the lofty rhyme.
>
> (3–11)

'Year' is disjoined from 'dear', even though lines 5 and 6 are also held together formally by a half-rhyme at the beginning; lines 6 and 7 are joined syntactically but they do not rhyme; lines 8 and 9 begin with a repeated pattern ('For Lycidas', 'Young Lycidas'). The syntax breaks line 10 in the middle and runs lines 10 and 11 together. Here the sense would lead us to expect a couplet but the rhymes refer back to lines 7 and 8. The effect is of feeling transgressing the austere discipline of the verse form, and the reader's attention is focused on the speaker's grief, which is brought under control with such difficulty. We are invited to attend in consequence to the subjectivity which thus marshals its feelings, the 'I' of line 3.

This 'I' is the main voice of the text. For much of the poem it is a doubtful, questioning voice. The occasion for a poem has come too soon. Why did no one intervene to save Lycidas? What is the value of poetry? Is it worth the struggle? Finally, however, the voice acquires authority. 'Weep no more, woeful shepherds weep no more' (line 165). The rhythmic echo of the opening line ('Yet once more, O ye laurels, and once more') declares this the moment of resolution. Lycidas is in heaven, where he hears the song of the saints.

But at the instant when, believing that we have been reading the direct utterance of the poet, encountering a subjectivity, Milton, we seem to share the triumph of his new-found confidence, 'Milton' slips away: 'Thus sang the uncouth swain . . .' (line 186). Another quite impersonal enunciating subject takes the place of the 'I' in the text, this time the author of a fiction in which an uncouth swain is the main speaker. An anonymous third-person narrative suddenly comes to frame the text we have read, turning it into a dramatic monologue, releasing the possibility of layers of irony. Where now is the (authorized) voice of *Lycidas*?

Meanwhile, there have been other voices, perhaps possessed of greater authority than the shepherd–speaker's. Phoebus Apollo speaks of true poetic fame. Quite apart from the Christian orthodoxy of his views, and his status as god of poetry, the weight and the finality of his concluding couplet convince us that he must surely be right:

> As he pronounces lastly on each deed,
> Of so much fame in heaven expect thy meed.
>   (83–4)

And the denunciation of bad poets by the 'dread voice' (line 132) of the pilot of the Galilean lake must certainly be right too, since his concluding couplet is even more solemnly resonant (whatever it means):

> But that two-handed engine at the door,
> Stands ready to smite once, and smite no more.
>   (130–1)

Who, then, is speaking in *Lycidas*? An uncouth swain struggling with the question of vocation? An increasingly confident Christian poet divinely endorsed by Apollo and St. Peter? A modern subjectivity desiring the Lacanian other (*objet a*) –

To sport with Amaryllis in the shade,
Or with the tangles of Neaera's hair?

(68-9)

Or perhaps an author desiring the Lacanian Other: longing to
be the origin of language, the source of meaning and truth, to be
able to inscribe the Word in the word, for ever in quest of
presence, but haunted by the lack which ensures differance?

2.3 Presence regained?

Paradise Lost marks a new start.

According to Dr Johnson, Milton 'was desirous to use English
words with a foreign idiom'.[10] There is a sense in which the
diction of all Milton's writing is international, though the
degree to which this is the case may have been exaggerated.
Alastair Fowler cites a comment of 1734 which is more to the
point than some of the subsequent debate:

> Milton's language is English, but 'tis Milton's English; 'tis
> Latin, 'tis Greek English; not only the words, the phraseo-
> logy, the transpositions, but the ancient idiom is seen in all
> he writes, so that a learned foreigner will think Milton the
> easiest to be understood of all the English writers.[11]

F. R. Leavis, for whom Englishness was more or less synonymous with virtue, would evidently have derived no pleasure
from the notion of the 'learned foreigner' with easy access to
Milton's work. In his view, 'cultivating so complete and
systematic a callousness to the intrinsic nature of English,
Milton forfeits all possibility of subtle or delicate life in his
verse.'[12]

As a result of Leavis's strictures on Milton's 'mechanical'
neglect of the lithe and sinewy movement of English idiom, and
the impoverishment of sensibility which is its inevitable consequence, Milton's admirers have tended to an uneasy defen-
siveness about his international style. Ricks urges that Milton
does after all value the intrinsic nature of English, 'and wishes us
to feel its power'.[13] Fowler concedes an element of Latinism
in *Paradise Lost* but argues that most of it is of the 'least

objectionable' kind, and could not be said to 'weaken the native sinews' of Milton's style.[14] The moralization of the debate (evidently non-English usage is culpable: what is in question is exactly *how* culpable Milton actually is) ignores a perhaps more interesting question, which concerns the implications of the foreign contours of Milton's writing.

R. D. Emma's analysis of Milton's grammar indicates that the classicism is not only a matter of vocabulary but is diffused through the texts. Gender, for instance, is assigned to neuter nouns 'often in accordance with Latin grammatical gender'; syntactic units within the sentence are marshalled with an economy modelled on Latin; sentence structure places the prose broadly within the Ciceronian tradition.[15] At the same time Emma stresses that many of Milton's now unfamiliar usages are entirely English, and surprisingly 'modern' into the bargain.

Not, of course, that Latin and Greek were irretrievably ancient in the seventeenth century. For the learned foreigner, as for Milton, the classical languages were still a going concern as a mode of communication. But Milton's internationalism was not exclusively classical. As F. T. Prince makes clear in *The Italian Element in Milton's Verse*, many of his most characteristic verbal patterns and larger poetic structures are cultivated directly from Italian Renaissance poetry. In conjunction with his debt to Shakespeare and Spenser, this seems to indicate that the project was to appropriate the most sophisticated, the 'highest' elements of all existing signifying practice.

If, as Johnson maintained, Milton 'wrote no language',[16] one of the reasons was that the central figures of his culminating work knew no nation. The protagonists of *Paradise Lost*, to the extent that the poem is a humanist epic, are man and woman, the representatives of a universal human nature. Humanism, as an emergent imperialism was to indicate, ultimately acknowledges no national frontiers, recognizes no cultural relativities. Its values are understood to be held in common, the secret or even unconscious desire of all peoples, and the whole world is its province. For humanism in its internationalist aspect cultural difference is no more than superficial, an affair, precisely, of the signifier. Beneath the differences of expression (since a developed humanism brings with it an empiricist theory of language) the reality of the signified is held to be the same in essence the world over. Ultimately it would become unnecessary to harness all cultures to demonstrate this fact: one's own, it appeared to British imperialists of the nineteenth century, offered all the required resources. But in the heady early days of the mid-seventeenth century the rich variety of existing signifying practice was the appropriate vehicle of universal truth.

But alongside the humanist epic, which recounts the emergence of human knowledge through the experience of tragedy, *Paradise Lost* offers another narrative, which Geoffrey Hartman calls its 'counterplot'.[17] Hartman finds in the account of Mulciber's leisurely fall from heaven an instance of God's divine imperturbability:

> from morn
> To noon he fell, from noon to dewy eve,
> A summer's day.
>
> (I, 742-4)

Providential control is there in much of the imagery of the poem, even in quite unexpected places, identifying as a major concern of the text the ways – or the will – of God.

Epics are master-narratives which define and delimit what is known and what is valued. They offer a mythological history which is above all an account of their own present. Social formations tend to produce them at their founding moments – Greece, Augustan Rome, Elizabethan England, and now post-Revolutionary England at the moment of the installation of liberal humanism. The project of epic is to fix the values (and not only the new values) of the society, to specify them as eternal essences and immobilize them in the heightened and decorated textuality of verse.[18]

If *Paradise Lost* records the emergence of humanism, it does so in the name of the divine will. At its heart, therefore, is once again the Logos, the ways of God, which in turn legitimate certain ways of men and women – and exclude others. In this sense all signifying practice – all language and all culture – is understood to be concentric, to centre on a single truth, to utter and reiterate the transcendental signified. Thus heterogeneous allusions – to the Bible, classical myth, patristic literature, English poetry and even the researches of Galileo – are assembled to tell what is in the end one story.

Satan, fallen into hell, wades through the sea of fire to the burning beach, and summons his former comrades:

> he stood and called
> His legions, angel forms, who lay entranced
> Thick as autumnal leaves that strew the brooks
> In Vallombrosa, where the Etrurian shades
> High overarched imbower; or scattered sedge
> Afloat, when with fierce winds Orion armed
> Hath vexed the Red Sea coast, whose waves o'erthrew
> Busiris and his Memphian chivalry,
> While with perfidious hatred they pursued
> The sojourners of Goshen, who beheld
> From the safe shore their floating carcasses
> And broken chariot wheels, so thick bestrewn
> Abject and lost lay these . . .
>
> (I, 300-12)

In twelve lines we learn very little about the specific condition of the fallen angels. But the multiple simile is by no means a digression.

Fallen leaves were a recurring simile for the dead. In the *Aeneid* souls waiting for Charon to ferry them to the underworld cluster on the shore as numerous as the leaves of autumn (VI, 309-10). In Dante's *Inferno* the same image reappears, moralized and Christianized: these are the souls who have died subject to the wrath of God (III, 112-15). Angels cannot die, but the allusion in Milton's poem indicates the analogy with their punishment, and the parallel foregrounds the absoluteness of divine justice.

Paradise Lost adds a specific location, Vallombrosa. This is a real place near Florence; possibly Milton had visited it. But at the level of the signifier the name would surely have suggested to Milton, who knew Italian well, the valley of the shadow (of death), and the image of God-as-Shepherd which the context of the metaphor evokes (Psalm xxiii). Providence too is part of the divine justice.

Orion belongs to classical mythology, but he had already been enlisted by medieval commentators as a symbol of God's power to raise storms to effect his punishments. The sedge (reeds), a visual image of the fallen angels, perhaps evokes the Red Sea at the level of the signifier, since the Hebrew name for it was 'Sea of Sedge'. In any case, the final analogy, this time from the Old Testament, again displays the vengeance of God, as the pride of the Egyptian army ('chivalry') is engulfed, in pursuit of the Jews, by the waters of the Red Sea. But here too the elect view the scene 'from the safe shore'. As Hartman points out, Providence ensures that hell is defeated even before Satan's voice is heard to rally the angels.[19]

The unnamed protagonist, then, of this triple epic simile, is God himself. The sequence of images offers an inter-textual, inter-cultural vista back through consecutive recorded instances of divine wrath and divine Providence. Bible narrative, classical epic and classical myth repeat what is finally a single story of God's ultimate mercy. The angels have put themselves beyond the reach of mercy, of course, but the addressee of the text is the human reader, who presumably has not, and who is invited to rediscover in a series of comparisons a single familiar truth. The simile acts as a demonstration of the ways of God throughout history.

In other cases the ways of God are defined by their difference. The image of Satan as Leviathan, a whale so huge that sailors have thought it an island, a place of safe anchorage (I, 200–8), notoriously elicited the withering irony of T. S. Eliot on the grounds of its irrelevance.[20] But the simile draws on the patristic tradition, which invokes this image of Satan's absolute untrustworthiness in contrast to the certainty promised by faith in God.[21] F. R. Leavis approved of the allusion to Proserpine gathering flowers: 'Her self a fairer flower by gloomy Dis/Was gathered . . . ' (IV, 270–1).[22] The parallel between Proserpine's innocent gardening and Eve's, which led to their capture by the King of the underworld, has become a commonplace of criticism. But Providence is there too in this allusion, even as the contrast is indicated between Eve's insouciance and God's care, made manifest in the resulting parallel with the Incarnation and the Atonement: 'which cost Ceres all that pain/To seek her through the world' (lines 271–2).

Thus all cultures and all narratives proclaim a single meaning-which-is-truth, conspire to justify the ways of God. And yet at the heart of the project there lies impossibility. Whatever words are invoked to define him, God cannot be contained there. He is beyond difference, and yet at the same time he is difference itself, able to be defined only in a succession of negatives: 'Immutable, immortal, infinite' (III, 373), 'invisible' (III, 375), 'inaccessible' (III, 377). God is different from everything we know, and therefore 'unspeakable', 'beyond thought' (V, 156, 159). The remedy is to recreate the song which inscribes the Logos, re-presents the transcendental signified, the song of the angels, the 'charming symphony' of heaven (III, 368). 'Thee Father first they sung' (III, 372): there is no distancing preposition between the song and its theme, its meaning, intention and referent. Music is irreducible, opaque, pure inscription. It is sound, pattern: it 'charms the sense'. The orisons of Adam and Eve incite the whole creation to sing, to declare God's goodness. Their praise takes the form of an appeal to angels, sun, moon and stars, to wind and water and all creatures to praise him in turn. The formula of their prayer (addressee + verb + 'his praise') thus constitutes a refrain for an elaborately patterned hymn which comes 'unmeditated' to unfallen lips (V, 145–204).[23]

And in its turn *Paradise Lost* too will sing:

> Sing heavenly Muse, that on the secret top
> Of Oreb, or of Sinai, didst inspire
> That shepherd, who first taught the chosen seed,
> In the beginning how the heavens and earth
> Rose out of chaos.
>
> (I, 6–10)

Paradise Lost itself will be the song of the muse, directly inspired by the same spirit who inspired Moses, shepherd of the Israelites in the wilderness, and archetypal poet. In heaven 'they sing the song of Moses the servant of God' (Revelation xv, 3), the song of triumph over the Egyptians swallowed up by the Red Sea while the Children of Israel were saved (Exodus xv, 1–19). In addition, Moses was the author of the Pentateuch, and thus the source of the creation epic itself, shadowing forth God's own works, 'In the beginning'. The phrase opens the book of Genesis: 'In the beginning God created the heaven and the earth.' It also opens St John's Gospel, where the citation of Genesis prepares for a reinscription by the New Testament of the relations between God and his creation: 'In the beginning was the Word.'

Paradise Lost thus traces its authority back through the most resonant moments of Scriptural poetry. But it will be more than a transcription of these earlier texts:

> I thence
> Invoke thy aid to my adventurous song,
> That with no middle flight intends to soar
> Above the Aonian mount, while it pursues
> Things unattempted yet in prose or rhyme.
>
> (I, 12–16)

Harnessing all cultures (the Aonian mount is the classical Helicon; 'unattempted yet in prose or rhyme' is an allusion to Ariosto), *Paradise Lost* is offered as a poem for its own moment and for all time. It calls on the aid of the Holy Ghost, who has always been present:

> And chiefly thou O Spirit, that dost prefer
> Before all temples the upright heart and pure,
> Instruct me, for thou know'st; thou from the first
> Wast present.
>
> (I, 17–20)

The poem, irreducible in its music, patterned, opaque, is to be more than a narrative of the events of the Fall. Itself a song, *Paradise Lost* claims to inscribe the ways of God.

2.4 Textuality

It cannot, of course, be done. Even in the opening lines of the poem differance divides song from song, authority from the author. 'In the beginning' (*Paradise Lost*, I, 9) is already a quotation, and thus a re-inscription, distancing the magnificent performatives of Genesis I and the sacred mysteries of St John from their echoes in the later text. It is the Muse who is to sing, but the text is also 'my . . . song ' (I, 13), the work of *this* human author. And the Holy Ghost can only in the end 'instruct' (I, 19), even though it is the Holy Ghost and not the author who was present. As in 'The Nativity Ode', the song which holds together God and his creation is necessarily human as well as divine, but this difference divides it from the 'unexpressive' music of the angels.

Paradise Lost cannot inscribe the Logos, because the inscription is always also a re-inscription, at one remove from the imagined plenitude of originary presence. In a similar way, the great hymn of the creation is made up of a series of echoes rippling out from the divine centre.[24] The angels 'circle his throne rejoicing' (V, 163); the sun praises God in its own sphere, its 'bright circlet' (V, 169). The sun sounds, the moon re-sounds (V, 178). The song of praise in the created world is a reiteration: its utterance is not primal, not unique. The prayer of Adam and Eve is already a re-petition.

The intertextuality of the epic similes has the effect of exposing the detour of the signifier. In the image of the fallen leaves (I, 301-4) the reference to Dante or to the Psalm is a signifier whose signified is another text, itself the (already-differed) signifier of God's justice. The list of earthly gardens which it is *not* distances Eden (IV, 268-85): 'Not that fair field/ Of Enna' . . . 'nor that Nyseian isle . . .' (268-9, 275). The classical allusions which elevate its perfection also diminish its reality, its certainty: 'Hesperian fables true,/If true, here only' (IV, 250-1). What emerges is the endless displacement of truth by the signifying process. The word is irretrievably fallen (X, 608); presence is differed and deferred.

But what also emerges in consequence is precisely the materiality of the signifier, the textuality of truth, the creativity of language itself. The 'charm' resides in the opaque surfaces of the text, the resonances, the patterns, and the process of production which makes meaning out of an assemblage of intertextual allusions, or out of the conjunction of English words and a foreign idiom. The writing of *Paradise Lost* is singularly dense, overtly producing meanings from the arbitrary nature of language.

For example, the text is full of puns. The serpent is 'voluble': 'coiled' in Latin, 'eloquent', or perhaps 'verbose' in English (IX, 436); for Beelzebub the inhabitants of earth are 'puny': weak and ineffectual in English, but in French *puis né*, born since the devils (II, 367).[25] The tree of knowledge is the 'root of all our woe' (IX, 645). And this allusion is rapidly followed by another but equally familiar form of Miltonic word-play: Eve tells the serpent that to have brought her to the tree is 'Fruitless to me, though fruit be here to excess' (IX, 648).

42 Poetry

The indeterminacy of meaning, the difference within the
signified, is put to work:

Blest pair; and O yet happiest if ye seek
No happier state, and know to know no more.
(IV, 774–5)

While there is a pun on 'know' and 'no', 'know' also differs
from 'know' by a hair's breadth, by the distinction between
understanding and possessing knowledge. Elsewhere the signifier slides, making connections at the phonetic level substantial
as 'evil' is linked with 'Eve', or 'fall' with 'false':

O Eve, in evil hour didst thou give ear
To that false worm, of whomsoever taught
To counterfeit man's voice, true in our fall,
False in our promised rising.
(IX, 1067–70)

Milton himself in his prefatory note to *Paradise Lost* drew
attention to the advantages of blank verse with 'the sense vari-
ously drawn out from one verse into another'. The strategy
permits surprise as an effect of the disjunction between syntax
and metre. The most famous example is probably the account of
the fall of Mulciber in slow motion through six lines, followed
by, 'thus they relate/Erring' (I, 746–7). The weight of 'erring'
depends on its unexpected place at the beginning of the line,
after the moment of apparent closure. Mulciber's 'fabled' fall
contributes its display of divine justice to the meaning of the
poem, but meaning is here explicitly divorced from truth. In a
similar disjunction of syntax from metrical pattern, Satan's
conscience

wakes the bitter memory
Of what he was, what is, and what must be
Worse.
(IV, 24–6)

John Hollander calls this a 'shocking . . . dissolution of the
linear facade'. 'Here the static pattern of line 25, framing the
formula from the prayerbook ("As it was in the beginning, is
now and ever shall be") is jolted by the revelation that "be"
was merely predicative (and of "worse" at that) rather than

existential.'[26] Closure occurs where it is least expected, fore-grounding once again the extent to which the signified is an effect of pattern and the disruption of pattern.

What is realized in the lists of alien names and exotic places, in the networks of international puns and intertextual allusions, in the surprises as well as in the verbal and metrical patterns of *Paradise Lost*, is not finally the Logos, but the primacy of textuality itself, not the presence of God but the triumphant presence of the signifier.[27] Meanings are made and remade, the signified is differed and deferred, with all the plurality and indeterminacy that that releases, not out of an originary encoun-ter, but out of other texts, out of the signifier, out of the endless creativity of language.

2.5 Transparency

But this was not, of course, the project. *Paradise Regained* once again tries something new. Despite much evidence of continuity with the style of the earlier epic, *Paradise Regained* is notoriously plainer and more transparent. It is less patterned, at least in its detail, and accordingly briefer, more laconic. The opening invocation of the Holy Spirit here is relatively terse, less allusive than the corresponding passage in *Paradise Lost*, and the text lays claim to no prophetic status. The point now is to narrate events, moving freely, in order to do justice to them, through the natu-ral world:

> inspire,
> As thou art wont, my prompted song else mute,
> And bear through highth or depth of nature's bounds
> With prosperous wing full summed to tell of deeds
> Above heroic.
>
> (I, 11–15)

And at once the story begins with John the Baptist crying in the wilderness and the baptism of Christ.

The discontinuities should not be overemphasized, of course. The final test in Milton's version of the temptation of Christ is the trial on the pinnacle of the temple:

> There on the highest pinnacle he set
> The Son of God; and added thus in scorn:
>   There stand, if thou wilt stand; to stand upright
> Will ask thee skill; I to thy Father's house
> Have brought thee, and highest placed, highest is best,
> Now show thy progeny; if not to stand,
> Cast thyself down.
>
> (IV, 549–55)

The difference within the signified is apparent again here: 'highest' first indicates a physical position, then supremacy; 'stand' only gradually reveals its challenge to Christ's 'skill', which is at the same time a test of his identity. But here the word-play seems to operate primarily as an instrument of the tempter's scorn: 'thy Father's house . . . highest is best . . . show thy progeny'. And the position of the reader, who knows the story and is already sure of Christ's progeny, is marked out in advance by the ironies of Satan's words. The effect of the puns is thus not in the end the release of meanings but convergence for the reader on a unified position from which they make a single point.

The climactic moment of this episode, and of the text as a whole, is narrated with the utmost simplicity:

> To whom thus Jesus: Also it is written,
> Tempt not the Lord thy God, he said and stood.
> But Satan smitten with amazement fell.
>
> (IV, 560–2)

The transparency is breathtaking. And as the text becomes fully expressive, the episode it records is itself a demonstration of the exteriority of the signifier. Christ stands and thus declares his identity. His divinity is an essence, veiled, but ready to be revealed at the right moment, to be signified. As signifier, the standing expresses an idea which is anterior to it, a condition of which standing is only the instrument. Reality and signification have become independent of each other, the signifier no more than an index of a truth which is elsewhere – and to which as a result it can never quite do justice.

The implication of both the narrative mode and the episode it narrates is that signifying practice is virtually transparent to the richness and complexity of an event, of meaning and truth (though I shall argue that this transparency is, finally, an illusion – see pp. 102–4 below). The event in its meaning and truth now has priority, and language, we are to understand, is no more than its instrument. Christ's divinity is knowable, but only at one remove, *through* language and not *in* it.

The fictional moment is one of triumph, but the textual consequence was to be the escape of both Christ and Satan, good and evil, from the net of language. These beings and these concepts were already receding into a realm of pure metaphysics beyond the reach of the signifier. As a result, the world of liberal humanism was released from the tyranny of the Church, an institution which set out to guarantee and thus control meaning and truth. In place of this, the modern world resigned itself to differance, to the isolation, the doubt and the unanswerable questions which are the effect of 'a relationship with that which we necessarily misconstrue', a signifying practice which pretends to transparency, but can never quite deliver the imagined plenitude of meaning-which-is-truth.

Is it possible in the twentieth century, as both the cultural relativity of humanism and the metaphysics of logocentrism become apparent, to glimpse a third option: that we might share the work of producing meanings – which are explicitly differed, deferred, plural, not anchored in a metaphysical tyranny, not an attempt to recover an ever-receding presence, not absolute – but meanings, nevertheless, by which to live?

3 Gender

3.1 Rape

Comus is about rape. The rape does not take place, of course, in a masque designed for family entertainment. The heroine is saved in the nick of time, thanks to the intervention of masculine virtue. The story is by no means unusual. Countless heroes from the classical period to the present have earned their place in myth and romance by rescuing maidens from the predatory sexuality of fabulous monsters or monstrous men. In the Christian tradition female saints have frequently been threatened with rape and tortured because they refused to submit. Alternatively, they are miraculously rescued, saved by Christ, the knight of heaven. The recurring tale of the helpless virgin depends on the recognition of female vulnerability, of widespread and apparently inevitable male rapacity, and of an ideal of masculine chivalry. In this sense the narrative has played its part in constructing two complementary stereotypes: for women feminine dependency and for men a virility which can be committed to good or evil.

Comus (*A Masque Presented at Ludlow Castle*) rehearses the familiar story, however, with a difference, and in consequence the text disrupts the established polarity between woman as natural victim and man as either predator or rescuer. In the masque tradition, where the thinnest of plots is conventionally adequate to the occasion, a romance narrative provides opportunities for the combination of song, dance, spectacle and moral philosophy which in the early seventeenth century reaffirmed for aristrocratic audiences their place in a harmonious cosmos. And yet in this specific masque it is precisely the imperatives of morality and poetic spectacle which interfere with the reaffirmation of the usual gender stereotypes. *Comus* resists the implications of its own plot.

This is doubly surprising in the context of the orthodoxy of the 1630s. In this period women were only very uncertainly subjects, barely allowed within the patriarchal order of language and culture a place from which to speak.[1] The emergent seventeenth-century redefinition of the family, which identified women as partners with their husbands in the construction of the home as a place of warmth and virtue, permitted wives to speak as long as they confined themselves to domestic issues. But the condition of their identification as subjects within the newly defined private world of the family was their exclusion from the public world of politics. The distinction between public and private was authorized by the Scriptures. St Paul had laid down that women should not speak in church: instead they should consult their husbands at home (I Corinthians xiv, 34–5). There were, of course, rejections of this prohibition, especially in the radical Christian sects, just as there were specific resistances to patriarchal social relations in general. But Richard Brathwait represented a wide section of orthodox opinion when in *The English Gentlewoman* (1631) he urged young women to be seen and not heard in the presence of their elders – or of men. When women were entitled to speak without impropriety, Brathwait argued, they should choose domestic topics. They should most certainly avoid politics and religion: 'to discourse of state matters will not become your auditory, nor to dispute of high points of divinity'.[2]

How extraordinary, then, that in 1634 it is the heroine who appears as the moral and political voice of Milton's masque, and that an addition in the 1637 printed text should show the Lady yet more eloquent, and the rapist in a cold sweat, acknowledging himself defeated by her words (lines 778–805).

In the hands of its most practised and accomplished exponents, Ben Jonson, who wrote the words, and Inigo Jones who devised the spectacle, the masque was an intensely moral and political form. In it aristocratic performers, resplendent in lavish and glittering costumes, displayed their virtue and their consequent right to rule, in a scenic entertainment which combined song, dance and dialogue.[3] The masque signified magnificence. Changes of scenery demonstrated a seamless mastery over the visual world; well-rehearsed dances emulated on earth the harmony of the spheres; and courtly compliment to the sovereign, or to the aristocratic figure presiding over the occasion, established the parallel between cosmic order and human social relations in their most perfect form. The masque showed the aristocracy an ideal image of itself. It thus offered instruction and reassurance simultaneously. Sumptuous visual effects joined with faultless execution to reveal a model of worldly control divinely endorsed.

But in the hands of Jonson's successors in the early 1630s the moral element in the masque was much reduced. The politics of the form became correspondingly more absolutist, the celebration of wealth and power more evidently divorced from the sense of moral obligation. Milton's masque is offered as a reaffirmation of the Jonsonian mode, a mirror of and for true nobility.[4] *Comus* was performed at Ludlow Castle to celebrate the appointment of the Earl of Bridgewater as President of the Council in Wales and Lord Lieutenant of Wales. The aristocratic performers were his three youngest children, Lady Alice Egerton, who was fifteen, John, aged eleven, and Thomas, aged nine. Lady Alice as victim, and John and Thomas as her rescuers, duly demonstrated both their virtue and their internalization of the proper sex-role stereotypes.

Comus himself, meanwhile, represents vice. His aim is to possess the Lady, by seduction or by force. As an emblem of revelry, riot, excess, however, in accordance with the Greek meaning of his name, Comus stands not only for lechery but also for the abuse of wealth and power. His arguments against temperance propose both sexual profligacy and conspicuous consumption, the use of riches for self-indulgence, personal sensual pleasure, empty display. Nature, he claims, is abundant, 'to please, and sate the curious taste' (line 713). 'Curious' here means fastidious, esoteric. Silk is the work of 'millions of spinning worms' labouring solely to 'deck' human beings in luxury (lines 714 and 716). Austerity – eating beans, drinking water and wearing wool – is an insult to the Creator, implying that he is parsimonious where in fact he is lavish (lines 720–5). Unless

Nature's produce is consumed, Comus goes on, it will over-
whelm the earth by its own ceaseless fertility. Without human
intervention birds would darken the sky, cattle take over the
world and diamonds burst out everywhere (lines 727–35). Both
wealth and beauty must therefore be spent on pleasure,

> must not be hoarded,
> But must be current, and the good thereof
> Consists in mutual and partaken bliss.
> (738–40)

Possibly. It does not follow, however, the contemporary audience might have reflected, that either wealth or beauty should be
dispensed indiscriminately. But since it is not self-evident (as
modern criticism has shown[5]) that these arguments in favour of
extravagance are false, it is imperative that they be countered
within the text. In their emblematic roles Comus is cast as vice,
the Lady as virtue. The responsibility is therefore hers. The
Lady apologizes: she had not meant to speak (lines 755–6). But
falsehood masquerading as reason cannot be allowed to triumph: 'I hate when vice can bolt her arguments,/And virtue has
no tongue to check her pride' (lines 759–60). And with this
explanation of what might otherwise appear a quite unfeminine
eloquence, she proceeds to put the case which constitutes the
moral and political message of the text as a whole. Nature's
abundance is not designed to encourage intemperance but to
ensure that with the proper distribution of wealth none need go
hungry:

> If every just man that now pines with want
> Had but a moderate and beseeming share
> Of that which lewdly-pampered Luxury
> Now heaps upon some few with vast excess,
> Nature's full blessings would be well-dispensed
> In unsuperfluous even proportion.
> (767–72)

What is more, she continues, she could if she wanted to give
an account of 'the sage/And serious doctrine of virginity', but
Comus is not fit to hear it (lines 783–6). Besides, she would
in the process be moved to such 'sacred vehemence' that the
earth would shake and bring down all the enchanter's magic

structures (lines 792–8). Comus recognizes his own moral defeat: 'She fables not, I feel that I do fear/Her words set off by some superior power' (lines 799–800).

The superior power is, of course, divine, the transcendental signified, anchor and guarantee of meaning and truth, the Logos, God. But its human mouthpiece is the Lady, cast as virtue resisting intemperance. Contrary to all expectation, in consequence of the moral and political imperatives of the text, the eloquence of a woman fuses word and Word, politics and religion, in a programme for personal virtue and the social organization of a Christian commonwealth.

Comus now abandons all hope of securing the Lady's consent and prepares to resort to force. At once her Brothers rush in with drawn swords and save the day, reasserting in the process the stereotypical relation between the sexes. The masque could well have ended here, with virtuous virility triumphant. But the formal and spectacular imperatives require a supernatural intervention. The occasion suggested a divinity representing the Welsh border, and since women are conventionally more spectacular than men, Sabrina, goddess of the river Severn, is brought in to effect the real rescue of her unfortunate sister, chaste and morally victorious, but physically glued to a chair in the enchanter's palace.

'Sabrina rises, attended by water-nymphs, and sings' (888 S.D.). The text gives no direct indication of the nature of the spectacle presented, unless we take the Attendant Spirit's invocation of the goddess to suggest her appearance and her costume:

> In twisted braids of lilies knitting
> The loose train of thy amber-dropping hair,
> Listen for dear honour's sake,
> Goddess of the silver lake
>
> (861–4)

The execution of the visual effects was not in the poet's hands. But the text continues to evoke visual images which presumably complement and extend what the audience actually sees. Luxuriant nature and precious gems specify and legitimate Sabrina's power:

By the rushy-fringed bank,
Where grows the willow and the osier dank,
    My sliding chariot stays,
Thick-set with agate, and the azurn sheen
Of turkis blue, and emerald green.

                                        (889–93)

The audience is invited to imagine in the Great Hall of Ludlow
Castle the velvet cowslips on which the goddess sets her 'print-
less feet' (lines 896–7).

But Sabrina also has a place in the moral structure of the
masque. Like the Lady, she was the daughter of a powerful
father, and she too was 'a virgin pure' (line 825). To escape
some not very clearly specified excess with broadly sexual connotations, Sabrina threw herself into the river Severn, where
water-nymphs took her in and bore her to Nereus. His daughters revived her and she was metamorphosed into a goddess.
The reason for Sabrina's flight is not recounted in detail:

The guiltless damsel flying the mad pursuit
Of her enraged stepdame Guendolen,
Commended her fair innocence to the flood
                                        (828–30)

The story is told in Geoffrey of Monmouth's *History of Britain*
and subsequently narrated by Spenser in *The Faerie Queene* (II, x,
17–19) and by Drayton in *Polyolbion*. In these three versions
Guendolen is the first wife of Locrine, who leaves her for Astrild.
The enraged wife has Astrild and her daughter drowned. In
Milton's version, however, the details are ignored, and the
earlier narratives are altered so that Sabrina is the agent of her
own escape. She herself commits her 'innocence' to the river.
After her transformation into a goddess she retains her 'maiden
gentleness' (line 842), and displays a special solidarity with
virgins threatened with rape,

For maidenhood she loves, and will be swift
To aid a virgin such as was herself
In hard-besetting need.
                                        (854–6)

The effect of this emphasis in *Comus* is to imply, without com-
pletely rewriting the narrative, that the 'mad pursuit' somehow

threatened Sabrina's chastity, and so to sharpen the parallels between Sabrina and the Lady.

When Comus first appears to the Lady in his own person she tries to rise from his enchanted chair. But she cannot do so. Comus tells her that he has the power to turn her to a statue, 'or as Daphne was/Root-bound, that fled Apollo' (660–1). The allusion to the story of Daphne and the rapacious Apollo is in practice no help to Comus, who is anxious at this stage to disguise his real intentions. Nor is the parallel at all exact. Daphne's roots were not a threat: on the contrary, they protected her from rape. But the reference can be read as helping to construct a network of relationships within the text between threatened rape, supernatural intervention and transformation. Daphne, the daughter of a river-god and Gaea, the Earth, aroused the desire of Apollo but fled from his embraces. In several versions of the story Daphne's mother turned her into a laurel tree as she ran to protect her chastity.[6] Both Daphne and Sabrina reinforce, therefore, one of the moral themes of the masque, that true virginity is the guarantee of special supernatural protection, whether by pagan magic or divine grace:

> So dear to heaven is saintly chastity,
> That when a soul is found sincerely so,
> A thousand liveried angels lackey her,
> Driving far off each thing of sin and guilt.
>
> (452–5)

The insistence that the human will to good ensures God's special protection, however threatening the external circumstances, is so important that the Attendant Spirit reiterates the point in the final lines of the text: 'Or if Virtue feeble were,/Heaven itself would stoop to her' (lines 1021–2).

But the network of meanings which links the Lady, Daphne and Sabrina inadvertently produces another set of parallels which lays *Comus* open to feminist reading. Daphne is saved by her mother; Sabrina is saved by the water-nymphs and the daughters of Nereus; and Sabrina saves the Lady. The point is never made explicit. But while the Brothers flourish their swords and the Attendant Spirit displays his abstruse knowledge, another drama of rescue is more quietly played out in the margins of the text. A series of female figures silently take it for granted that they have a responsibility towards each other, and that there is a special kind of support in that unobtrusive and unsurprising relationship between women. It is because of what they have in common, the text implies, that Sabrina is able to release the Lady. The real protagonists in Milton's drama of projected rape, the agents of virtue, the subjects of the text in every sense, are women, after all.

3.2 Sexuality

But in case this should appear to be an effect of Milton's deliberate intention, an expression of his sympathy for what we should now call feminism, *Samson Agonistes* offers a useful corrective. Dalila is no Lady, but an inveterate enemy of virtue, lascivious, treacherous, destructive. A 'serpent', a 'viper' (lines 997, 1001), Dalila is the wife who betrayed the secret of her husband's strength to his enemies. She is the source of his present suffering and struggle, cause of the 'agon' of the title. Samson calls her 'That specious monster, my accomplished snare' (line 230) and the intensity of his hatred is registered in the density of the vocabulary. 'Specious' is both false and fair-seeming; 'accomplished' indicates her gifts, her accomplishments, and at the same time specifies the closure of the trap she lured him into.

But it is the Chorus who are most vehement in condemning Dalila, and who most generalize her crime:

> wisest men
> Have erred, and by bad woman been deceived;
> And shall again.
>
> (210–12)

No doubt this observation would have been enough to evoke for a seventeenth-century audience lists of wicked women who had betrayed good men: Helen of Troy and Clytemnestra, Cressida and Cleopatra, Jezebel, Salome and, of course, Eve. The context is always sexual. Frequently such women are endowed with voracious erotic appetites or demonic sensual attactions of a kind few normal men could resist. But they often seem to suffer from a corresponding under-development of their moral and intellectual faculties. The Chorus reflect on what must have been a familiar question:

> Is it for that such outward ornament
> Was lavished on their sex, that inward gifts
> Were left for haste unfinished, judgement scant,
> Capacity not raised to apprehend
> Of value what is best
> In choice, but oftest to affect the wrong?
>
> (1025-30)

(Paradoxically, if the Chorus had attributed these errors in the construction of femininity to culture rather than nature, they might have been making a radical point. Within a few years women themselves would begin to protest that their rational and ethical capacities were not raised by an education which trained them only in the feminine arts and denied them access to Latin, Greek and Hebrew.[7])

Poor Samson has been unfortunate in his marriage choices. His first wife extracted from him the answer to a crucial riddle 'in her height/Of nuptial love' (lines 384-5), and Dalila sold his secret in the midst of her 'spousal embraces' (line 389). It is this betrayal of marriage which incites the Chorus to the greatest bitterness. But this too is seen as a common occurrence: once she is installed in the home, the gentle bride all too often turns out a virago, or worse:

> Seeming at first all heavenly under virgin veil,
> Soft, modest, meek, demure,
> Once joined, the contrary she proves, a thorn
> Intestine, far within defensive arms
> A cleaving mischief, in his way to virtue
> Adverse and turbulent, or by her charms
> Draws him awry enslaved
> With dotage, and his sense depraved
> To folly and shameful deeds which ruin ends.
>
> (1035-43)

The imagery of the wife as a thorn in the flesh, an enemy deep within the fortress of her husband's arms, stresses the intimacy of marriage. The metaphor which follows identifies it as a shared journey in which the partners, though not equal, are expected to pull in the same direction: 'What pilot so expert but needs must wreck/Embarked with such a steers-mate at the helm?' (lines 1044-5). Truly happy marriage is rare: it is also infinitely precious (lines 1046-9).

The new meaning of marriage which emerged in this period aroused the highest expectations. No longer merely a remedy for lust, or a way of perpetuating the dynasty, marriage became in the seventeenth century what it still is for many: a union of minds in the exclusive bond of true love, the guarantee of mutual support and harmony, a source of virtue defying and deflecting the harsh competitiveness of the world of work and politics. This utopian ideal is one of the main themes of Milton's divorce tracts, published in the early 1640s. Marriage is seen as a spiritual union, a knitting of souls for the avoidance of loneliness. Procreation is secondary, a consequence of love itself. The real purpose of marriage is 'the communicating of all duties, both divine and human, each to other, with utmost benevolence and affection.'[8] (It is for this reason, Milton argues, that divorce by consent of the parties ought to be permitted: once the harmony of souls is lost, the marriage is in reality at an end, and no external legislation can preserve it.) In a sonnet not published until 1673 the poet dreams of his 'late espoused saint': 'saint', presumably, because the dead wife is now in heaven, but also as an indication of her disposition (XIX, 1). For the same double reason she appears 'vested all in white, pure as her mind' (line 9). She has no visible body (she is a spirit, the poet is blind), 'yet to my fancied sight,/Love, sweetness, goodness in her person shined' (lines 10-11).

There is, however, a price to pay for the spiritualization of love and marriage. The higher the ideal, the more carefully the boundaries of sexuality are policed and the more rigorously improper desires are excluded. In this dualism of mind and body, love which is located first in the mind is alone legitimate, the proper foundation of family life, and this love is separated off from the lusts of the body, which are seen as animal. One of the most celebrated of all hymns to marriage occurs in *Paradise Lost*, and here both the dualism and the policing are strongly in evidence:

Hail wedded love, mysterious law, true source
Of human offspring, sole propriety
In Paradise of all things common else.
By thee adulterous lust was driven from men
Among the bestial herds to range, by thee
Founded in reason, loyal, just and pure

(IV, 750–5)

It is not, of course, that desire is excluded from marriage. But what is admissible is a sexuality brought under the control of the mind, purged of all that is arbitrary, momentary, contingent. True love is purposive, deliberate rather than accidental. It measures reason, loyalty, justice, purity. It resides, *Paradise Lost* continues, in marriage, and not

in the bought smile
Of harlots, loveless, joyless, unendeared,
Casual fruition, nor in court amours
Mixed dance, or wanton mask, or midnight ball.

(IV, 765–8)

The arguments of the Lady in *Comus* against indiscriminate sexuality have now crystallized into a series of explicit prohibitions.

It goes without saying, since its proper location is marriage, that true love is also heterosexual, and that it depends on a recognizable difference between the sexes. The difference between men and women is not, of course, merely anatomical: it is a difference of mind, of demeanour, of disposition. In Milton it is also a difference of authority. In the interests of good order men, more rational, more *self*-controlled, are naturally put in charge (*Samson Agonistes*, lines 1053–60).

Dalila transgresses the ideal in every way. She is all body. She has lured Samson into 'pleasure', 'voluptuous life', 'venereal trains' (lines 533–4). She substitutes treachery for intimacy, betrayal for mutuality. Now she weeps false tears and offers domesticity without concord, marriage without unity. But above all she has the effect of inverting the proper hierarchy and disturbing the accepted system of sexual differences. Throughout the text Samson castigates himself for his surrender to Dalila's sexuality, laments the 'impotence of mind' that led him to be overcome by female importunity (lines 50-2). His fault is 'weakness' (lines 50, 235, 834), a 'servile mind' (line 412). Dalila has 'vanquished' him (lines 235, 562) where whole bands of Philistine warriors would not have dared to take him on (lines 1110-15). He was 'yoked', enslaved by her (lines 410-11) and now it is fitting that he is literally enslaved by the Philistines (lines 38-42). He is redeemed only when he obeys instead the will of God, who alone deserves men's submission.

The cause and consequence of his surrender to Dalila is lack of manhood (line 408), lack of mastery of his own desire. He has been 'effeminate' (lines 410, 562), uncontrolled, like a woman. The imagery of inverted values, authority overturned and sexual difference in disarray culminates in the picture of Samson's head in Dalila's 'lascivious lap' (line 536). Here mind submits to body, strength to sensuality, masculinity to a whore. Samson is shorn of his hair and turned out, weak, 'ridiculous' and 'disarmed', 'like a tame wether' (a castrated ram) (lines 537-40).

Ironically, all this has the effect of placing the major share of the blame on Samson. Of course, the moral project requires that Samson is responsible for his own sin and thus merits his punishment. And he is, after all, the central figure of the drama, so it is his temptation and fall which are charted in most detail. The result, however, of this textual emphasis on Samson's weakness is a play which throws into relief the fact that while women are dangerous, men are vulnerable, susceptible to an anarchic desire, an inadequately moralized sexuality. What makes its appearance within Samson's marriage is the irrational, impure, bestial lust which betrays men to their own ruin. Dalila is hardly more than the occasion. The real thorn intestine, the mischief within his own defences, is the masculine vulnerability which delivers his rightful control into her hands.

Power is always precarious, maintained only by effective policing. At the heart of *Samson Agonistes* is an account of marriage as a struggle for power, in which men dare not relax their vigilance for an instant, in case they lose control not so much of women but of themselves. The relative irrationality of women, their anarchic sexuality, while it legitimates male authority, is at the same time the force which threatens it. The differences of disposition and of authority between men and women are precisely the source of instability in what should be permanent, of warfare in what ought to be perfect harmony.

Samson Agonistes leaves us to construe that this is so only when women are evil, that female wickedness in a fallen world is the precipitating cause of marital strife and masculine error. *Paradise Lost*, however, pursues the same question – and comes to a rather different conclusion.

3.3 Reading Graves reading Milton

Robert Graves's novel, *Wife to Mr Milton* (1942), is the story of Marie Powell, who at sixteen became Milton's first wife.[9] The story opens with Marie's gift for her fifteenth birthday from her godmother. It is a book bound in white vellum with a lock and key, but to Marie's surprise the pages are blank. Her godmother explains: Marie, with her lively fancies and inventions, is to write her own book. She already has a talent for telling stories, but this is to be a different kind of story, the record of her own life. Marie's record, inscribed in the white book with its virgin pages, is of course the basis of the first-person narrative we are reading. Ironically, it is Milton's wife who, despite her lack of learning, makes out of her own vitality and her own experience the shrewd, witty and courageous story of love and war and patriarchy which offers the reader so much pleasure.

Marie has to apply to her father for pens and ink. He agrees to provide them when she allows him to write something of his own on the title page. He draws the family coat of arms, and colours in this emblem of dynasty with his own blood. The scandal of Marie's life-story, the novel makes clear, is that she is to be the property of men. She is an object of exchange, married in the interests of one family to produce another. Her father marries her to Milton to redeem a debt. Milton desires her for her long golden hair, but he treats her without sympathy because she refuses to submit to his will and because her marriage portion is not paid. The women – Marie, her mother and her servant, Trunco – are the strong, caring, effective figures in the story. Marie's father is financially incompetent, her husband sexually and domestically inept. She retains her independence and her wit throughout the narrative.

Wife to Mr Milton is thus a fictional denunciation of Milton's sexism. As such, it is in a sense a reading of Milton's texts, including of course the divorce pamphlets and *Samson Agonistes*, but perhaps above all of *Paradise Lost*. No feminist in her senses would try to find anything cheerful to say about Milton's myth of male oppression divinely ordained. The poem itself notoriously proclaims its own patriarchal reading of the almighty Word. Adam and Eve are explicitly (and repeatedly[10])

> Not equal, as their sex not equal seemed;
> For contemplation he and valour formed,
> For softness she and sweet attractive grace,
> He for God only, she for God in him.
>   (IV, 296–9)

His very appearance signifies 'absolute rule' (IV, 301), hers 'coy submission' (IV, 310), since her image bears less resemblance to God's (VIII, 543–4). The obligation imposed on Eve as a result of the Fall to subject her will to Adam's (X, 195–6) is hardly a punishment, since the requirement was there all along.

The feminist critique of *Paradise Lost* goes back at least to Charlotte Brontë's *Shirley*. Its history is traced by Sandra Gilbert and Susan Gubar in *The Madwoman in the Attic*, where Milton is identified as the aesthetic patriarch a series of women writers have had to overthrow in the anxiety of anti-feminist influence.[11] None the less, there are recent instances of feminist appropriation of *Paradise Lost*,[12] and I want to contribute to this process of rereading, on the basis that the text can be seen at certain points to exceed the utterances of its own narrative voice. If *Paradise Lost* is not a feminist text – and it certainly isn't – it can still, I believe, be read on behalf of feminism. And Graves's novel, more subtle and more incisive than the official literary criticism of its period, helps perhaps in spite of itself, to illumine what is dark in Milton's epic.

Wife to Mr Milton seeks to construct Milton's personal views as the explanation of *Paradise Lost*'s portrait of Eve, treating in fiction Milton's fictional text as the transcription of the poet's (warped) experience. The 'truth' of Milton's married life is also the truth of the sexism of *Paradise Lost*, the *Adam Unparadised* which Milton is shown in the novel forever drafting, never actually writing in Marie's lifetime. The novel endorses Marie's independence, her sense of adventure and her wit, denouncing by reversing it the epic's ideal of coy submission.

But the plot of *Paradise Lost* depends, of course, precisely on the failure of this submission, on the self-assertion and independence of 'adventurous Eve' (IX, 921). Shoshana Felman, who draws a parallel between criticism and the psychoanalytic transference, points out that it is the unconscious of the reading which reappears in the critical writing. When the patient transfers to the analyst repressed feelings of love or hate, it is the unconscious which acts out or repeats the nature of the original relationship. In the same way, in Felman's analysis, the critical reading re-enacts an unconscious relation to the text, an interpretation it does not consciously acknowledge. It thus reveals the plurality of the text itself.[13]

Paradise Lost, I have suggested, is two texts in one, an absolutist poem, which struggles to justify the ways of an authoritarian God, and a humanist narrative, which recounts how human beings become free subjects, knowing the difference between good and evil in a world of choice. The Fall is a liberation as well as a catastrophe (see pp. 82–4 below). As the knowledge of difference, and the installation of the lack which is the condition of desire, the Fall produces subjects who, knowing the external world, are promised as its *other* the plenitude of a paradise within them, happier far (XII, 587). The emergence into difference is thus the triumph of humanism, and Eve, who resists the patriarchal absolutism of God and Adam, is its cause. The equally irrepressible heroine of *Wife to Mr Milton* thus constitutes an unconscious repetition of the poem's own (unconscious?) account of Eve.

Paradise Lost is an epic poem, but the central figures of the emerging humanist text are beginning also to be identifiable as characters in a novel. Though their individuality tends to be masked by the epic voice they all share with the narrator, the text includes what seem to be moments of pure *vraisemblance*, when their speech or behaviour can be read as expressive of an idiosyncratic interiority.[14] At such moments the figures appear endowed with a life which exceeds their representative epic status. If this is true of Eve, it is possible to see how Graves, reading the epic as narrative fiction, might find in Eve the basis of the novelistic character he attributes to Marie. Both Eve and Marie have golden hair which reaches to their waists (IV, 304–5; pp. 41, 173). Both are outspoken, though capable of self-control. Both, of course, defend their freedom. Is Eve also witty?

It seems unlikely that Eve would be permitted to make a joke. Epics are no laughing matter. And yet the behaviour of the newly created Eve, read as if it were an episode in a novel, at once presents itself as comedy. Drawn to look into the lake, she sees an image which bends to meet her:

> I started back,
> It started back, but pleased I soon returned,
> Pleased it returned as soon with answering looks
> (IV, 462–64)

Moments later she sees Adam for the first time. This image is far less agreeable than the one in the lake. Again she starts back – until Adam persuades her to return and recognize his superior 'manly grace' (IV, 490). The account of Eve surveying Adam, finding him unappealing and turning back resolutely to her lake-mirror is an unexpected twist in the story which is pure delight. The comedy depends on the symmetry between the two events: each time she looks, starts back, returns to the image. It also depends on our knowing what the new-born Eve does not: that lakes are looking-glasses, that men are sexy in a *different* way. And yet it is Eve who retrospectively recounts all this to Adam, deliberately drawing attention to her own ingenuousness in a piece of innocent sexual teasing which places her as simultaneously knowing and naive. Adam smiles at her story (IV, 499). And so, perhaps, when he read it, did Robert Graves, who unconsciously found in the work of the poet he denounced the character of the heroine his novel offers for our admiration.

The advent of humanism and the novel, like the redefinition of marriage as a partnership, did not, however, spell the dissolution of patriarchal relations, but only their rearrangement. Women were still the *opposite* sex, everything that was not masculine. If the moment of sexual differentiation allows Eve a voice, it is none the less precisely a *differentiated* voice, charming, erotic, experiential. Adam smiles 'with superior love' (IV, 499) as his bride makes winning comedy out of her own artlessness. When Adam records the same incident it is not comic, but moralized and theorized, and the voice is rational, analytical, masculine. Eve's hesitation is now defined as the effect of

> innocence and virgin modesty,
> Her virtue and the conscience of her worth,
> That would be wooed, and not unsought be won.
>
> (VIII, 501–3)

According to Shoshana Felman's analysis of criticism as transferential repetition, the critical reading also unconsciously repeats what it denounces in the text. In this sense *Wife to Mr Milton* acts out the sexism it condemns in *Paradise Lost*. Marie is a writer too, and it is her comic and observant narrative which offers the reader the immediate pleasure of the novel. This pleasure is precisely experiential and, of course, sexual. (If the high point of the romantic story is Marie's night in the church with her Royalist lover, the high point of the comedy is certainly her wedding night with her puritan husband.) It is the detail Marie provides, the sheer accumulation of *vraisemblance*, creating the illusion of real experience artlessly recounted, which makes the novel and its narrator so engaging.

Marie has a voice, but it is a voice which in the end is stereotypically feminine. The voice of Milton, the poetry itself, meanwhile, is always located at one remove from the everyday domesticity of the narrative. Milton's poetic gift is debated but never seriously called in question. The epic voice, we are left to conclude, is representative, analytical, portentous . . . masculine. Despite its good intentions, *Wife to Mr Milton* ultimately reaffirms the patriarchal values it denounces.

And yet the novel too exceeds its own conscious project, its humanist quest for the author as origin and explanation of the nature of the text. In practice the pompous Mr Milton explains nothing of the quality the novel finds in his poetry. The fictional Milton's learning is barely more than pedantry, his theology esoteric, his understanding of human affairs minimal. But there is something more in the poems, a mysterious remainder which Marie recognizes but cannot quite define. How could so stunted a character be the author of such writing – unless the author is not the explanation of the text?

In this respect the novel goes beyond the explicit views of its own author. In his critical essay, 'The Ghost of Milton', written five years after the novel in 1947, Graves made his own judgment of Milton's poetry luminously clear. Milton, he declared, was fundamentally interested in nothing but 'hacking his way to the Temple of Fame over the dead bodies of his enemies, rivals and friends'. 'With all possible deference to his admirers, Milton was not a great poet . . . He was a minor poet with a remarkable ear for music' – until he grew bloated with Satanic ambition and wrote an epic. Of *Lycidas* Graves wrote, 'the sound of the poem is magnificent; only the sense is deficient.' But Milton's musical craftsmanship has lulled generations of readers into unintelligent acquiescence.[15]

Where the essay is pure mischief and excellent comedy, the novel is more serious. *Wife to Mr Milton* does not discuss *Paradise Lost* directly, since the epic was not written until after Marie's death, but it replaces the essay's monologic mastery and dismissal of Milton's poetry with a dialogue on *Comus*, between Marie and her brother James, which enlists the reader in unresolved debate. Here James makes the accusations levelled in the essay, but with less comedy and more hesitation. He is 'troubled' by the discrepancy between the poet's manifest ambition and the poem's sureness of touch. James says of Milton, 'he is more passionately set on literate fame than in love with poetry itself. Yet, by God, I have no flaw to find in a single line.' Marie, meanwhile, is fascinated by the argument in *Comus* about chastity, as well as by the verses 'with their serpentine mazes of sound'. James the moralist (like Graves the critic) finally denounces the ambition: 'The more that a poet regards Fame, so much the less will he regard Truth.' But Marie the fellow-writer rejects this criterion of judgment: 'I had not thought that it was for poets to speak truth, which is rather left to the divines and philosophers to expound.' It is the textuality of the text which delights her, the elusiveness of its pleasure, the undecidability of its meaning. Marie is not lulled into mindless acquiescence by Milton's poetry: she is excited (pp. 94–7).

James and his creator look for the single, authorized truth of the text – and do not find it. But fiction, which leaves truth to the divines and the philosophers (and, we might add, to the critics), offers a more illuminating reading of Milton's texts than a criticism which, demanding the message, represses or denies the textuality and so misses the (sliding) meanings.

3.4 Sexual difference and power

As fiction, *Wife to Mr Milton* refuses to fix the meaning of *Comus*.
Similarly, *Paradise Lost* as fiction magnificently fails to fix the
meaning of sexual difference, whether in absolutist or in
humanist terms, and so the poem uncovers what it cannot
explicitly acknowledge, the precariousness which is an inevitable effect of power. Patriarchal power is not an essence of
masculinity or femininity but a relation of difference. It is a
mistake, however, to suppose that the *other* which defines power
is its antithesis. What power masters is not itself powerless, or
where is the mastery? Power, to *be* power, needs not submission
but resistance, which constitutes a form of rivalry. Thus patriarchy, which locates the defining difference as sexual, constructs
sex itself as a place of instability, of threat. Samson is lost when
he lays his head in Dalila's lap. At the heart of patriarchy is a
deep fear of women's sexuality, not as its cause but as its effect.

Paradise Lost knows this, though the knowledge runs counter
to the assertions of the narrative voice. In Book VIII Adam and
Raphael labour to reason it out. The sexual act, Adam con-
fesses, is 'the sum of earthly bliss' (line 522), transporting him
beyond the condition of serene superiority which is the result of
all other pleasures. Here alone he is 'weak/Against the charm of
beauty's powerful glance' (lines 532–3). He knows, of course,
that Eve is really inferior (line 541), but her 'loveliness' makes
her appear 'absolute', so that what she wills seems best (lines
547–50). Raphael tells him that what so transports him is no
more than 'an outside' (line 568). With skilled management Eve
will yield appearances to reality and acknowledge Adam as her
head (lines 573–5). God rightly made her powerful: so beautiful

> for thy delight the more,
> So awful, that with honour thou mayst love
> Thy mate, who sees when thou art seen least wise.
>
> (576–8)

She is lovely for his pleasure; she is awe-inspiring to be worthy
of his love; and she will be there to see if he shows any weakness
or folly (cf. IX, 312–14). The last phrase is condensed and oddly
contorted ('sees', 'seen'). Above all, Adam should not give way
to passion, which will betray his control (VIII, 585, 588, 635–6),

make him weak against beauty's power. Thus the argument completes a circle. What emerges from the discussion does little to vindicate male authority. The stress is all on Adam's vulnerability, as it was on Samson's. In *Paradise Lost* love is seen as a power struggle in which both partners keep Adam under perpetual surveillance, continually examining him for signs of weakness. The danger is that he may surrender to Eve's sexuality, the potent force which necessitates and justifies patriarchal mastery.

This time, however, unlike Dalila, Eve is no viper, but the innocent creature God has made. The beauty that makes her worthy of Adam is also what makes her dangerous and therefore in need of management. The paradox is evident in the poem's description of her hair. Adam wears his long, but not below his shoulders (IV, 301-3). Meanwhile, to signify sexual difference,

> She as a veil down to the slender waist
> Her unadorned golden tresses wore
> Dishevelled, but in wanton ringlets waved
> As the vine curls her tendrils
>
> (IV, 304-7)

Eve's hair is like a veil covering her unclothed body, a signifier of propriety, of sexuality subdued. And yet it has an intense sexual life of its own as it waves in wanton ringlets, dishevelled. Later, she leans her naked breast against Adam, 'under the flowing gold/Of her loose tresses hid' (IV, 496-7). 'Loose' here can be read as investing the covering with precisely the sexuality it is there to conceal.

Graves and the editor of the standard edition of the poems both take this as evidence of Milton's special sexual preoccupation with hair. There is no need. The meaning of women's hair as at once a glory and a danger, a covering and a temptation, both modest and seductive, goes back at least to St Paul (I Corinthians xi, 15, 5, 13), and was reaffirmed by a succession of Renaissance moralists. A veil ensuring decency, an ornament, it should none the less be kept covered as a danger to men.[16] Botticelli's Venus, whose heavy tresses offer a minimum of covering even as they enticingly escape their confining ribbon in the sea breeze, is a descendent of the mermaids who lured sailors to their death by combing their long, concealing, tantalizing golden hair among the waves. The shepherd–poet of *Lycidas* is not fetishistic in his momentary longing to abandon asceticism for 'the tangles of Neaera's hair' (line 69). Its beauty is both a glory and a snare.

Eve's unfallen sexuality is at once God-given and dangerous. The instability is not individual but representative: this is what men, to be masters, must subdue, and it is precisely their ability to dominate such a powerful force that legitimates patriarchal control. The achievement of mastery is, we are to understand, a perpetual struggle, difficult enough to be worth winning. Thus power produces fear, not as a psychological consequence but as a structural one. This is the relationship between men and women ordained by a patriarchal God.

The consequence, of course, is the Fall. Adam submits to his own susceptibility: he subjects his wisdom to female charm and his will to Eve's. What is strange is that God apparently learns nothing from the event. After the Fall he simply reinstates the same patriarchal relations which brought it about (X, 195–6), and the whole cycle of fear and failure, of surveillance and self-assertion, is repeated throughout history.

Or perhaps not. The text does envisage a possible solution. At the end of their discussion Raphael tells Adam with a disarming blush that there is love in heaven, and there the angels simply mix freely in perfect union, without all these difficulties (VIII, 618–29). In the heaven he speaks of, however, there are, of course, no women (X, 889–90).

This arrangement might not do for us. But *Paradise Lost* also offers the basis of a more utopian vision. Though the angels are identified by masculine pronouns throughout, and are thus presented as essentially male, the text none the less draws attention to the fluidity of heavenly gender: 'For spirits when they please/ Can either sex assume, or both . . .' (I, 423–4). Either . . . or both: not simply a sexual duality, a bisexual ability to move between antithetical poles, nor a uniform androgyny, but an internalization of difference itself, of sexual otherness within the self-same.

Milton's plural angels are by no means unique. Italian Renaissance painting, too, often shows God's emissaries as sexually ambiguous. Annunciating angels, for example, are commonly placed in a relationship of spatial and pictorial symmetry with the Virgin, their physical characteristics resembling hers to

a surprising degree. How strange that a culture which so polar-
ized male and female stereotypes should represent a higher form
of life as thus transgressive, apparently endorsing sexual
undecidability.

The effect in the paintings is the divorce of sexual difference
from its alliance with power. Neither Gabriel nor the Virgin lays
claim to mastery. And in Milton's heaven there are no gender
stereotypes, no antithetical voices, masculine and feminine, no
opposition affirmed as privilege. There can be, in consequence,
no sexual rule and no submission, no authority grounded in
anatomy.

The text goes no further than this. But in separating gender
from anatomy, and in glimpsing the possibility of a difference
within sexual identity, *Paradise Lost* allows its reader a
momentary vision of a world beyond essences. The result is
imaginable as sexual plurality for each individual, and the consequent release of sexual being from power.

God ought to have thought of that. It would have made all the
difference in the world.

4 Sovereignty

4.1 God

God is absolute plenitude, full, continuous and eternal; he is the first and the last; he is unequalled, without similitude. God is complete, without lack: 'Thou in thyself art perfect, and in thee/Is no deficience found' (*Paradise Lost* VIII, 415–16). He is 'uncircumscribed' (VII, 170). In the beginning he is everything and everywhere, total, unlimited presence: 'Boundless the deep, because I am who fill/Infinitide, nor vacuous the space' (VII, 168–9). He is unconstrained, absolute power: 'what I will is fate' (VII, 173).

Such plenitude exists only in the imaginary world of undifferentiated totality. Without difference God is also without meaning, outside the symbolic order which is the order of language and culture.[1] Ironically, he makes these claims, declares himself the absolute 'I am', at the heart of a written text, an epic poem which in turn aspires to be the inscription of the universal symbolic order, which harnesses all languages and all cultures to justify the ways of God. And the epic in *its* turn derives its authority from the divinely authorized Scriptures, the written exposition of God's ways.

It is precisely in terms of the Word that God enters the symbolic order. The Word, begotten Son of the Father (VII, 163), is God's image (VI, 736), the signifier of the transcendental signified, expression of an essence which is itself 'unspeakable' (V, 156), 'beyond thought' (V, 159). It is by means of the Son that God enters into the realm of signification, becomes perceptible:

Begotten Son, divine similitude,
In whose conspicuous countenance, without cloud
Made visible, the almighty Father shines,
Whom else no creature can behold; on thee
Impressed the effulgence of his glory abides,
Transfused on thee his ample Spirit rests.
(III, 384–9)

'Made visible', 'impressed', 'transfused': the terms define a relationship which is so close, so intimate as to be indivisible (like the recto and verso of a sheet of paper, as Saussure describes the relation between signifier and signified). *Paradise Lost* struggles with this mystery of the connection between the Father, only begetter of his own image, and the Son who is, who inherits and who participates in God's glory, and who affirms, 'Thou shalt be all in all, and I in thee/For ever' (VI, 732–3). The debate in Heaven in Book III, which echoes the debate in Hell, is in practice no debate at all, since the Son only utters what the Father already knows:

Son of my bosom, Son who art alone
My word, my wisdom, and effectual might,
All hast thou spoken as my thoughts are, all
As my eternal purpose hath decreed.
(III, 169–72)

But the Son's words are not redundant: they need precisely to be *said*.

Between the signifier and the signified there is proximity, intimacy, similitude, but also difference, spacing, however infinitesimal. The Son is not identical to the Father. The *Christian Doctrine* is emphatic on this issue, insisting that God is one, singular and unique, while the Son is his image, God made visible.[2] In *Paradise Lost* the Son is God's interlocutor, his executor and his substitute. It is the begetting of the Son that constitutes the inaugural difference which endows God with meaning and identity. The Creation follows: heaven and earth are differentiated, peopled; the earth is filled with different kinds of living creatures. God becomes a subject, the Creation the object of his power, his knowledge and his care.

God is signified in the Son, and one of the meanings specified in that image is love:

> in him all his Father shone
> Substantially expressed, and in his face
> Divine compassion visibly appeared,
> Love without end.

(III, 139–42)

Love reaffirms the unity of the differentiated Father and Son, reunites the Creator and his Creation. But love itself is also inevitably differential, a relation between the subject who loves and the loved object. As the object of desire, loved by the beings he has created, God is recognized, reaffirmed in his completeness and perfection, acknowledged and praised. Thus mirrored in the gaze of his Creation, God becomes whole again, recovers his imaginary plenitude, transcends difference. But as the subject who loves, God is at the mercy of the division, which haunts all subjects, between the 'I' who speaks and the 'I' who appears in the utterance. It is this difference within subjectivity, the inability to be fully present in the signifier, which initiates desire. Like all subjects, God is subject to desire, which is always in the end the desire for the acknowledging, affirming, mirroring desire of the other. Only the gaze of another subject can give back to God the imaginary plenitude of perfect presence, reasserting his unity as speaker and spoken, signifier and signified, the absolute 'I am'. God wants to be loved.

But because the plenitude of presence is always precisely imaginary (beyond difference and without meaning, unutterable and thus finally unthinkable), desire can never be fulfilled. So it is with God's desire. Paradise is always already lost, even to God. The objects of desire are infinitely interchangeable in an endless succession of displacements, because what animates desire is not the love of a specific other, but the lack within the speaking subject, the aspiration to be in control of the symbolic order itself, to be both source and signifier of meaning, and thus fully present in the 'I am'. In Lacanian terms, 'desire is the desire of the Other', desire to assume the place of meaning, and for that reason it finds in the end only absence:

> the subject, in articulating the signifying chain, brings to light the want-to-be, together with the appeal to receive the complement from the Other, if the Other, the locus of speech, is also the locus of this want, or lack.

That which is thus given to the Other to fill, and which is

strictly that which it does not have, since it, too, lacks
being, is what is called love.[3]

Such desire is necessarily insatiable. The Creation is supplied
with infinitely fine gradations of difference, 'various forms'
from plants to angels (V, 473–90). Even so, the desire of God
can never be satisfied: the multiplication of loving subjects is
also the multiplication of differences, and thus the replication of
sites of desire.

4.2 Obedience

The various forms which inhabit the cosmos also represent
'various degrees', more refined and more spiritual as they are
nearer to God. The Creation is profoundly hierarchic. The
angels are disposed in different orders, possessing degrees of
power. All are required to bow before the Son who is their head
(V, 606–8). At the end of Book III Satan succeeds in concealing
his identity from Uriel by 'bowing low' – 'As to superior spirits
is wont in heaven,/Where honour due and reverence none
neglects' (lines 736–8). In Paradise hierarchy is even more pro-
nounced. Adam and Eve are not equal to one another, but in
relation to other created things they are 'lords of all' (IV, 290).
The purpose of their one restraint, the arbitrarily forbidden
tree, is to signify that they accept their place in a hierarchic order
dominated by God. The divine prohibition is

> The only sign of our obedience left
> Among so many signs of power and rule
> Conferred upon us, and dominion given
> Over all other creatures that possess
> Earth, air, and sea.
>   (IV, 428–32)

The absolute 'I am' requires absolute obedience as evidence
of love. In this way, the whole Creation becomes a mirror,
reflecting back God's total power and his infinite goodness. The
universe, filled with his will, is to reaffirm his plenitude, even in
its difference. But there is an important resemblance, *Paradise
Lost* insists, between obedience and love: the acknowledgement
of his sovereignty, like the recognition of God as an object of
desire, gives him pleasure only in as much as it is freely yielded.

Both praise and submission please only on condition that they
are an effect of choice. God is quite clear and explicit about this:

> Not free, what proof could they have given sincere
> Of true allegiance, constant faith or love,
> Where only what they needs must do, appeared,
> Not what they would? What praise could they receive?
> What pleasure I from such obedience paid,
> When will and reason (reason also is choice)
> Useless and vain, of freedom both despoiled,
> Made passive both, had served necessity,
> Not me.

$$(\text{III, } 103\text{--}11)$$

The point is evidently important. Raphael reiterates it in detail
to Adam in Book V (lines 525–34), and then summarizes its
application to the condition of the angels:

> freely we serve,
> Because we freely love, as in our will
> To love or not; in this we stand or fall.

$$(\text{V, } 538\text{--}40)$$

Love is love only if it can be withheld, or devoted to another
object; power is power only if it can be resisted. This does not
imply that resistance is necessarily successful, of course. But it
must be an option. You don't in the normal sense of the term
have power over an object – a turnip, or a writing-desk. Love is
within the capacity only of a subject who recognizes difference,
and chooses *this* object and not another; sovereignty is held only
over subjects capable of choosing not to submit.

God's sovereignty, *Paradise Lost* affirms, is good. Obedience,
like love, is therefore an effect of free and rational choice. The
freedom of the angels and of human beings to stand or fall is a
recurrent preoccupation of the text. God made Adam and Eve
'Sufficient to have stood, though free to fall' (III, 99). The
double alliteration here creates a symmetry between the two
parts of the line: the equal alternatives are held in balance by the
pivotal 'though', which concedes the choice. As for the angels,
'Freely they stood who stood, and fell who fell' (III, 102). In this
instance the symmetry between the syntactic repetitions ('stood
who stood', 'fell who fell') emphasizes the equality of the options
which specify the nature of freedom. But at the same time the
antithesis ('stood', 'fell') stresses the difference between

the options, the difference within freedom, which is also the difference that defines freedom, since freedom to stand is also and necessarily freedom to fall.

Only a subject can choose, can serve God and not necessity. But the subject is constituted in difference, in division from itself, as the condition of its place in the symbolic order. It is this division within the subject which is the location of desire. Subjects can desire God, but they can equally desire what is not God. They can, for instance, desire to take the place of God. Thus Satan, envious of the Son's pre-eminence, and believing himself injured by it, withdraws from God his love and his obedience, resolves to 'leave/Unworshipped, unobeyed the throne supreme' (V, 669–70). The new object of Satan's desire is Sin, who springs out of his own head and represents a perfect image of him (II, 755–65).

The begetting of Sin is evidently a parody of the Son's generation. This episode, we are to understand, is the moment of Satan's reconstitution in difference, when he takes up his new place in the symbolic order and jubilantly (mis)recognizing himself in his own (desired and desiring) mirroring other, supposes himself present in the 'I am'. It is as a consequence of this imaginary autonomy that Satan denies his creation by God. He claims that he is 'self-begot, self-raised' (V, 860), and that his power is his own, not God's gift (V, 864). Meanwhile, the union between Satan and Sin produces Death.

Adam's initial desire for Eve is not sinful: it too is evidence of his freedom. God is 'not displeased' when Adam asks for a companion (VIII, 398). The birth of Eve from Adam's rib is yet another allegory of the division which constitutes the subject. Eve too is made both in Adam's image and as his other, 'Manlike, but different sex' (VIII, 471). Once again the inaugural difference endows Adam with identity, with subjectivity. It also leads to the Fall, when Adam confronts the choice between conflicting objects of desire, and opts for Eve, his other, differentiating self, rather than God:

> So forcible within my heart I feel
> The bond of nature draw me to my own,
> My own in thee, for what thou art is mine;
> Our state cannot be severed, we are one,
> One flesh; to lose thee were to lose my self.
>
> (IX, 955–9)

The Fall brings death into the world.

The condition of power, its meaning and its difference, is the ability of its subjects to choose another object of desire and to withhold obedience. Without that capability both Satan and Adam, the text insists, would have served necessity, not God. Sovereignty produces (the possibility of) resistance as its defining other, its visibility.

4.3 The elimination of difference

In *Paradise Lost* desire is free and its objects may be right or wrong. The wrong choice leads only to intensified absence, intensified desire. The quest for false objects leads in human beings to the final emptiness of death, while the superhuman figures, who cannot die, waste in the eternal privation of hell.

Misplaced desire is figured in the poem as oral. In Eden eating the arbitrarily forbidden fruit is a signifier of disobedience, of desire deflected from God. The satisfaction is only momentary and the taste is mortal. Eve greedily devours the fruit, delighting in the physical pleasure, as well as the expectation of knowledge and the hope of godhead. She eats without restraint, not realizing that she is 'eating death' (IX, 792). Meanwhile, Death himself, who devours human beings as his prey, pines, nevertheless, with 'eternal famine' (X, 597–609). Hell, too, is indestructible hunger and unquenchable thirst. When the devils take possession of the garden, they fall upon the fruit of the tree of knowledge, believing that it will allay their insatiable appetite. But the fruit turns to ashes in their mouths, and their desire is only rendered more acute, more desperate. Hell itself is represented as having perpetually 'ravenous jaws' (X, 637).

Ultimately, misplaced desire in turn consumes its subject. Satan confronts the absolute privation of his fallen condition in a metaphor which echoes (or anticipates) and parodies God's claim to absolute plenitude ('Boundless the deep, because I am who fill/Infinitude', (VII, 168–9):

> my self am hell;
> And in the lowest deep a lower deep
> Still threatening to devour me opens wide.
>
> (IV, 75–7)

For Satan the lack which is the ground of desire defies conception, just as infinity escapes human imagination. He carries absence within him, and the lowest depth of this internal hell still opens (impossibly) on further vacancy. Only desire itself is indestructible. If God cannot create a world which is sure to satisfy him, Satan, by refusing to love and to obey, chooses to enter a world where the fulfilment of desire endlessly recedes, to the point where the void invades and consumes his own being. The inaugural difference, the constitutive division within the subject, is prised open to such a degree that subjectivity itself begins to disintegrate. Satan, who aspired to take the place of God, recognizes that he himself is the source of his own destruction. This recognition is part of his punishment. The self-consuming process can never come to an end, but since the fallen angels cannot die, it can never be completed. The moment of recognition is one of despair, 'All hope excluded' (IV, 105).

The alternative, as Satan perceives it, is to seize control, to assume the place of the Other, and so transcend difference and desire. Rather than give up the struggle, he renews his former assertion of imaginary mastery, resolving to take charge of meaning in order to take possession of hell: 'The mind is its own place, and in itself/Can make a heaven of hell, a hell of heaven; (I, 254–5). In the event this radical subjectivism proves to be over-optimistic: the symbolic order is not at the disposal of the individual. Meaning, however plural, is public and conventional, not a matter of private choice. Satan's claim that he can remake the meaning of hell depends on his illusion of the sovereign subject: 'What matter where, if I be still the same?' (I, 256). His project is to eliminate difference and its implications by identifying the subject as the origin of meaning. In Book IV he reiterates the attempt, and more succinctly: 'Evil be thou my good' (line 110). This is exactly the rhetorical structure by which Adam rationalizes his choice of Eve rather than God, of death in preference to life: 'if death/Consort with thee, death is to me as life' (IX, 953–4). The willed elimination of difference is an attempt to restore imaginary plenitude, placing the subject beyond the symbolic order and beyond desire, and in the process legitimating whatever choice the individual makes.

The divine project, God's providential plan for the fulfilment of desire, is the ultimate elimination of difference in another (but related) sense. If Satan carries a devouring hell within him, Adam and Eve are to posses a paradise within which keeps at bay the hardships of external reality (XII, 587). This privileged realm of harmony, filling and fulfilling the desiring interiority which is the essence of the subject, separated off from all that is disordered or beyond control, foreshadows the final condition of the cosmos. In the end, when God repossesses his Creation, there will be no more division, and in consequence no more sovereignty: 'For regal sceptre then no more shall need,/God shall be all in all' (III, 340-1). God and the Son and the faithful will be held in perfect unity within a restored plenitude which is synonymous with the divine identity, the 'I am': 'Thou shalt be all in all, and I in thee/For ever, and in me all whom thou lovest' (VI, 732-3). As an effect of God's will, there will be no trace of the dividing, depriving, devouring difference, no remnant of unsatisfied desire, and no more power. Earth will be 'changed to heaven, and heaven to earth,/One kingdom, joy and union without end' (VII, 160-1).

But the inaugural difference cannot be transcended by an act of will, not even the will of God, since will is precisely an aspect of subjectivity and therefore an effect of difference. The price of plenitude restored, of unity freely chosen, and sovereignty abolished, is the fixing of difference as final and absolute. As a condition of the union of heaven and earth for ever, the damned are relegated to hell, to eternal privation. The instability which is the effect of difference, the precariousness of a world determined by desire, can be overcome only by cementing difference as opposition and eternizing the lack. Heaven and earth are made pure and new not by eliminating difference but by sealing off all that is other in hell (X, 637-9). The Last Judgment is the act of a despot, however benevolent.

4.4 Truth

Truth is the means by which free, rational subjects are recruited to love and to obey. Recognizing the truth, choosing it in accordance with reason, they naturally observe its imperatives. The trouble with truth, however, is that it always seeks a metaphysical anchor, locates its guarantees beyond the order of language, in nature, science, consciousness, or God, and these concepts act as guarantees only to the extent that they are themselves beyond question, given. By this means truth comes to deny difference and to operate as a mode of control.

Adam and Eve as knowing subjects are in a position to possess a paradise within. Knowing the difference between good and evil, they are able precisely to differentiate, to choose rightly, to recognize 'that which is truly better' and in consequence to obey the will of God:

> And perhaps this is that doom that Adam fell into of knowing good and evil, that is to say of knowing good by evil . . . He that can apprehend and consider vice with all her baits and seeming pleasures, and yet abstain, and yet distinguish, and yet prefer that which is truly better, he is the true warfaring Christian.
>
> (*Areopagitica*, pp. 514–15)

Reason, which is synonymous with the power to choose (*Areopagitica*, p. 527; *Paradise Lost* III, 108), endows human beings with a sufficiency which enables them to choose rightly. A person of great piety, challenged on the grounds that he read scurrilous books, heard the voice of God say, 'Read any books what ever come to thy hands, for thou art sufficient both to judge aright and to examine each matter' (*Areopagitica*, p. 511).

Areopagitica, Milton's attack on censorship printed in 1644, is one of the founding and canonical texts of modern liberalism. It defines a humanist subject who, perpetually confronted by choice, learns by experience to distinguish truth from falsehood. The text retains its resonance in the twentieth century as a passionate declaration of the fundamental right to freedom of thought and speech: 'Give me the liberty to know, to utter and to argue freely according to conscience above all liberties' (p. 560). It is equally modern and equally forthright in its commitment to tolerance. In a world in which there is so much to know, and so much desire to know, there will inevitably be much debate, many opinions: 'there must be many schisms and many dissections made in the quarry and in the timber ere the house of God can be built' (p. 555). Precisely because the ultimate project is unity, it is important in the mean time to tolerate difference: 'Yet if all cannot be of one mind – as who looks they should be? – this doubtless is more wholesome, more prudent and more Christian, that many be tolerated, rather than all compelled' (p. 565). Of course, there are limits: no one could be expected to tolerate popery, superstition, impiety, evil . . . (p. 565). Thus the boundaries of liberal tolerance begin to be marked and policed. The location of the boundaries will change with time, of course, but the existence of boundaries themselves is a constant feature of liberalism.

Within this rather authoritarian version of tolerance, however, the text begins to glimpse a broader, more inclusive pluralism. For a moment in *Areopagitica* truth is not merely a matter for debate, its singularity the final object of a knowledge based on the exchange of views. On the contrary, truth momentarily becomes plural. The possibility is an effect of the doctrine of 'things indifferent' to salvation. If, as St Paul argues, certain activities, like the observance of the old law, for instance, are a matter of genuinely free choice, having no implications for salvation, specific customs, conventions or actions may be either right or wrong indiscriminately, a question of individual preference. Truth, then, 'may have more shapes than one. What else is all that rank of things indifferent, wherein truth may be on this side or on the other, without being unlike herself?' (p. 563). Not realizing this, the sects are warring, expelling one another, failing 'to keep truth separated from truth, which is the fiercest rent and disunion of all' (p. 564).

The possibility that truth might be plural is glimpsed only briefly in *Areopagitica*. And even here the concession is no more than pluralism – the acknowledgement of plurality in things that hardly matter, that leave the existing framework of values essentially unchallenged. For most of the text truth is seen as single, however fragmented – and the occasion of conflict. The task of warfaring Christians is to reassemble truth's scattered limbs and defend the dissected body of their martyred saint (pp. 549–50). As in *Paradise Lost*, salvation is an effect of right reason, the correct choice, recognition of the truth.

But at the individual level how are we to be sure that we recognize the truth? This, of course, is where the conflicts start. The problem is dramatized in *Paradise Lost*. Surrounded by conspirators, Abdiel clings to what he believes and speaks out boldly against the planned revolt. Abdiel, faithful among the faithless,

gets it right (V, 896-903). But equally individually Satan gets it
wrong. When the Son is anointed, Satan mistakenly thinks himself impaired (V, 665). We know that he is wrong because the
narrative makes it clear to us, but how is Satan himself to tell?
What, in other words, are the grounds of true knowledge?
Abdiel knows, for instance, that the existing order must be right
and providential because God created the angels and gave them
their degrees in the hierarchy; and what he knows, he says, he
knows on the basis of God's goodness, and he knows *that* from
experience (V, 809-48). Satan, however, rejects Abdiel's case –
on the grounds that the specifically relevant experience is not
available:

> who saw
> When this creation was? Remember'st thou
> Thy making, while the maker gave thee being?
> We know no time when we were not as now.
>   (V, 856-9)

Satan succeeds in persuading one group: God retains the allegiance of the rest. Thus parties are formed and a contest for
power begins.

Satan has a point. Abdiel believes that God made him on the
basis of authority, not experience. (Knowledge based on experience would not amount to very much.) God himself is the only
guarantee of the truth that he defines. The narrative voice
reaffirms that truth for the reader: we recognize the truth of the
fiction on the authority of the text. There is thus an inherent
authoritarianism in a world where truth, specified as single,
constitutes the difference between right and wrong. There is also
an inherent instability in such a world. Truth, invoked to unify
free subjects in the recognition of authorized knowledge, in
practice produces dissension and division. *Areopagitica*, which
takes the dissension for granted, proclaims the inevitable triumph of truth: 'Let her and falsehood grapple; who ever knew
truth put to the worse in a free and open encounter?' (p. 561).
Paradise Lost, the product of a less heartening moment of history,
tells a rather different story.

4.5 Interest

The Tenure of Kings and Magistrates, written in 1649 to justify the execution of Charles I, introduces a new contestant in the wars of truth. This figure is identified as political interest. It was a feature of the English Revolution that both sides invoked the divine plan to guarantee the justice of their own cause: both King and Commons acted in obedience to God. Each side, therefore, naturally accused the other of the deepest hypocrisy. *The Tenure of Kings and Magistrates* draws attention to the evasions and equivocations of those members of the clergy who, constantly shifting their ground, claim to act on behalf of Providence, and in practice serve their own interests. For them there is no truth, no right action in the absolute sense, but only what their own advantage defines as right and true. On the other hand, when their interests are not involved, they are nowhere to be found:

> But if there come a truth to be defended, which to them and their interest of this world seems not so profitable, straight these nimble motionists can find no even legs to stand upon, and are no more of use to reformation throughly performed, and not superficially, or to the advancement of truth . . . than if on a sudden they were struck maim and crippled.
>
> (pp. 255–6)

Similarly, it is interest and not conviction which motivates the wicked to support the rule of tyrants. Evil people love licence, not liberty, and licence flourishes under tyranny. Such people are always ready with words like 'loyalty' and 'obedience' to justify their own collusion with corrupt rule (pp. 190–1).

Thus, although interest is identified consistently as the opponent of truth and justice, the text can nevertheless be read as beginning to recognize the extent to which political choice is in practice politically motivated. *The Tenure* does not, however, take the logical next step, and offer to enlist the opposition in its own cause by addressing their interests. The text is full of enemies: apart, of course, from the dead King, there are the wicked, the Presbyterians, all those who disagree with the text, and finally 'the obdurate enemies of God and his Church'

(p. 238). *The Tenure* does not, as it might, set out to recruit its opponents by presenting the state of affairs it defends as serving their interests (though it takes for granted that what it defends is generally beneficial). On the contrary, it lambasts them for their wickedness and folly. The rhetoric of truth is ultimately divisive: 'no man who knows aught can be so stupid to deny . . .' (p. 198); 'no understanding man can be ignorant that . . .' (pp. 231-2). To reject the argument is to place oneself as stupid or ignorant. 'Nor let any man be deluded by either the ignorance or the notorious hypocrisy and self-repugnance of our dancing divines' (p. 195). The argument by sneer and dismissal is the less acceptable face of the Enlightenment devotion to reason and truth. (Though the practice makes supporters of the cause feel good, it has very little to do with either reason or truth in the usual sense of those terms.[4]) Reason *should* unite all who disagree. Manifestly, however, in practice it does not. Those who dispute what the text proclaims as truth are therefore either knaves or fools. Thus liberal humanism consistently re-enacts the battle to convert interests (plural) into truth (single – and authoritarian).

The Tenure of Kings and Magistrates glimpses the possibility that political conviction and political allegiance are effects of political choice. It confines this to the wicked, however. Bad people are politically motivated: good people recognize what is true. But when *Paradise Lost* addresses the same issue, the analysis is more complex.

Eve succumbs to temptation and falls on the basis of lies. The serpent's argument is in many ways exceptionally plausible. It is apparently based on experience: 'Look on me,/Me who have touched and tasted' (IX, 687-8). It resembles the argument of *Areopagitica* (pp. 514-15): 'if what is evil/Be real, why not known, since easier shunned?' (*Paradise Lost*, IX, 698-9). Moreover, it appeals precisely to reason: 'And wherein lies/The offence, that man should thus attain to know?/What can your knowledge hurt him?' (IX, 725-7). No wonder the serpent's words seem to Eve to be rational and true (IX, 738). To counter them she has only the real truth, based on (arbitrary) authority, God's command (IX, 652).

Nevertheless, we are to understand that Eve chooses what is false in preference to what is true. Is she wrong?

Adam, on the other hand, falls on the basis of interest. He does not doubt or debate the truth. On the contrary, he considers what he wants:

How can I live without thee, how forgo
Thy sweet converse and love so dearly joined,
To live again in these wild woods forlorn?
Should God create another Eve, and I
Another rib afford, yet loss of thee
Would never from my heart.

(IX, 908-13)

Adam eats the forbidden fruit, 'Against his better knowledge, not deceived' (IX, 998). He knowingly and deliberately chooses Eve before God, human society in preference to divine allegiance. Is he wrong?

Lovejoy's essay, 'Milton and the Paradox of the Fortunate Fall', was first published in 1937, and since then it has been widely accepted that the notion of the Fall as a *felix culpa* can be traced back at least to the seventh century, and perhaps earlier. Christian history could not tolerate the possibility that Adam and Eve had genuinely frustrated God's providential plan. It was consequently necessary that the Fall be incorporated into the divine comedy as paradoxical in its implications. On the one hand, therefore, it was a disaster, the first disobedience and the cause of all our woe, but on the other it was a fortunate event, the occasion of a display of God's love in the Incarnation and the Atonement, source of the redemption of human beings into bliss.[5]

All this, a Lovejoy points out, is indicated in *Paradise Lost*. In Book XI Michael unfolds the catalogue of human miseries which is an effect of the Fall. But his narrative ends with the rainbow after the Flood, the sign of a convenant between heaven and earth, and Adam rejoices (XI, 865-9). When Michael describes the Incarnation, Adam is overcome with joy (XII, 372-3). After the Last Judgment, Michael declares, the earth will all be paradise, and far happier than the garden (XII, 463-5). Thus God reverses Satan's 'Evil be thou my good', but this time without eliminating the difference. The Fall is an evil act out of which Providence produces good (XII, 470-1).

And for Adam and Eve, to the extent that this is a humanist

text, the Fall is the condition of their full entry into the symbolic order. Knowing good and evil, knowing the difference between good and evil, they are only now full humanist subjects, full participants in the order of language and culture. Satan promised Eve that they would become 'as gods/Knowing both good and evil' (IX, 708–9). They do become as gods: God says so, though he maintains that they are not happier (XI, 84, 88). But when Michael has explained it all to Adam, so that he knows the meaning of the Fall, it is made clear that he need only add deeds appropriate to his new knowledge in order to possess a paradise within him 'happier far' than the external paradise he leaves behind (XII, 581–7). The Fall is thus a triumph for humanist interiority, that essence of the humanist subject which is the realm of its true being, its real autonomy, and a triumph for the individual in full possession of reason and truth. The final lines of the poem are the inscription of the end of a tragedy which is also the beginning of an adventure:

> Some natural tears they dropped, but wiped them soon;
> The world was all before them, where to choose
> Their place of rest, and providence their guide:
> They hand in hand with wandering steps and slow,
> Through Eden took their solitary way.

> (XII, 645–9)

Free to choose, together ('hand in hand') and independent ('solitary'), no longer subject to a single and arbitrary command, though with Providence on their side, Adam and Eve set out into the world which is 'all before them'.

The condition of possessing a paradise within is the knowledge of truth (and deeds to prove it). Adam finally makes clear that he has grasped the one truth that really matters: 'Henceforth I learn, that to obey is best,/And love with fear the only God . . . ' (XII, 561–2). And Michael agrees: 'This having learned, thou hast attained the sum/Of wisdom' (XII, 575–6). The affirmation of this truth is the project of *Paradise Lost*. But truth, Milton's texts demonstrate, is ultimately no less authoritarian than the original arbitrary imposition of the one restraint. Truth operates at the level of the signifier just as surely as does the forbidden tree. Adam learns the truth from what Michael tells him; that Michael tells the truth is guaranteed by God. The reader learns the truth from *Paradise Lost*; that the epic tells the truth is guaranteed by the authority of the narrative voice, by the Muse, by the Scriptures, by God. Ultimately, only God can hold the truth in place, authorize it against alternative knowledges produced by free subjects. This truth, the texts reveal, cements difference as opposition; it identifies its opponents as knaves and fools; it condemns the damned to hell. Truth is a despotism. It enlists subjects in obedience to an authority which needs no other justification.

As a master-narrative (perhaps the greatest ever), *Paradise Lost* proclaims the truth.[6] But within the text, its implications not fully developed in the mid-seventeenth century, there resides an alternative analysis, another way to choose, another politics. At the climactic moment of the story, the moment of the critical choice between allegiances, Eve, not knowing the truth, chooses falsehood, and Adam, undeceived, chooses according to his interests. Their choice deconstructs the binary opposition between truth and falsehood, good and evil. They choose humanity, not God, but God is not finally repudiated (identified as a knave or a fool, banished). On the contrary, in the final image of the poem Adam and Eve have each other *and* Providence. Their choice releases difference in place of antithesis: it demonstrates that alternatives need not be exclusive.

The Fall is the moment when human sovereignty is first glimpsed as a possibility. It is no more than a possibility while truth holds sway. Interest masquerading as truth always excludes its others – other interests – insisting that there is no alternative. But *Paradise Lost* points to a way of enhancing human sovereignty, by substituting for the politics of truth, anchored in metaphysics, a politics of interest, which is also necessarily, since interests are always plural, a politics of difference.

5 Narrative

5.1 Subjectivity

In the 1640s subjectivity became a major theme of Milton's writing. The inner realm of the Cartesian subject, whose thought is a condition of existence, who exists precisely as consciousness, is a territory explored and peopled in the course of the sixteenth and seventeenth centuries. The nineteenth-century view that it was also discovered in that period implied that it was there from the beginning of time, awaiting only the intrepid voyagers of the Renaissance, equipped with the maps and charts of a new humanist knowledge. In *The Subject of Tragedy* I argued an alternative case: that interiority was created in the moment that it was colonized, produced and populated simultaneously in the major discursive shift which founded the modern humanist epoch. It is humanism itself which proclaims its own world view eternal, beyond cultural difference, available and ready to be 'recognized' by other less fortunate cultures.

The inner space of subjectivity, which came into being in the Renaissance, and which declares itself the inalienable right of all human beings, is capable of becoming for those who choose virtue a paradise within. Interiority is the location of choice, and in consequence of freedom. The kingdom of the mind is a place of retreat from outward tyranny, of course, but the mind that loves virtue also naturally loves political freedom. On the other hand, this inward liberty, freedom of conscience, is inevitably freedom to love vice, and in consequence to opt for despotism. This is the story of *The Tenure of Kings and Magistrates*. The protagonists are 'men within themselves' (p. 190), born free but, until the execution of the King, enslaved. Those governed within by reason love good and liberty: they are now in the ascendant. But those who freely submit to custom and blind affections, 'slaves within doors', prefer tyranny, since it licenses evil and thus conforms to 'the inward vicious rule by which they govern themselves' (p. 190). These people constitute a perpetual threat to political freedom. The consciousness of individuals, 'men within themselves', determines history.

Reason and the right of the subject to choose are the theme of *Areopagitica*, and in this text it is possible to glimpse something of the fixity which comes to characterize the humanist definition of subjectivity. The warfaring Christian struggles, like Spenser's knights in *The Faerie Queene*, against the temptations of a fallen world (*Areopagitica*, p. 516). And yet Milton's Christian is in possession of an inward stability unknown to the heroes of the text written fifty years earlier. Unlike Guyon, who moves through a thrilling and frightening world and is accordingly tempted or troubled, the true warfaring Christian of Milton's text, 'sufficient both to judge aright and to examine each matter' (p. 511), already possesses an inner adequacy which precedes all temptation and which promises victory over evil. And conversely, unlike the Red Cross Knight, who falls into the depths of Orgoglio's dungeon and can still be rescued, the wicked of *Areopagitica* may be already armed from within against their own redemption: 'Banish all objects of lust, shut up all youth into the severest discipline that can be exercised in any hermitage, ye cannot make them chaste that came not thither so' (p. 527). Consciousness determines conduct.

In *Paradise Lost* the concern with subjectivity sits uneasily with the epic mode. It is perhaps an effect of history that twentieth-century readers tend to find the inner conflicts of the central figures more interesting than the war in heaven. We are, after all, a culture preoccupied by the self. To a critical tradition steeped in character-analysis, much of the pleasure of *Paradise Lost* lies in the glimpses it offers of an interiority which is not on display in earlier epic poems:

> So spake the apostate angel, though in pain,
> Vaunting aloud, but racked with deep despair.
>
> (I, 125–6)

Here, as in *Areopagitica*, a silent, brooding consciousness precedes and determines experience. For the fallen Satan this state of mind is the 'torment' which transforms all places into the hell he carries within him. Here he is in Eden, addressing the newly created Earth:

> With what delight could I have walked thee round,
> If I could joy in aught, sweet interchange
> Of hill, and valley, rivers, woods and plains,
> Now land, now sea, and shores with forest crowned,
> Rocks, dens, and caves; but I in none of these
> Find place or refuge; and the more I see
> Pleasures about me, so much more I feel
> Torment within me, as from the hateful siege
> Of contraries; all good to me becomes
> Bane.
>
> (IX, 114–23)

We are invited to delight in the romance landscape, generalized as shores and forests, rocks and caves, and engaging to the degree that we draw on other fiction to supply the connotations of these geographical features. But the intensity of the passage for the reader depends on the difference between outer and inner: our pleasure in the account of what is there for all to see is contrasted with the privilege of access to a private sphere of torment which, we are to understand, is shown to us but concealed from the other figures in the fictional world of the poem. And our access is doubly privileged in that the passage assumes the supremacy of the subject over its surroundings. Satan's state of mind dominates and determines his relationship to the landscape.

It also determines his actions: 'For only in destroying I find ease/To my relentless thoughts' (IX, 129–30). Satan's subjectivity is the secret which explains all our woe, a secret which the narrative voice shares with the reader, offering us a special knowledge, a special insight into the workings of the moral universe.

Naturally (which is to say, culturally), the secrets of the subject are presented in direct speech, in the first person, their truth guaranteed by the proximity of the speaking voice to consciousness. What Satan utters (makes outer) is what is *in* his head: he 'from inward grief/His bursting passion into plaints thus poured' (IX, 97–8). And the impression of authenticity is heightened when the rhythms of the verse cut across the formal and metrical pattern, echoing the 'spontaneous' rhythm of speech:

> Revenge, at first though sweet,
> Bitter ere long back on itself recoils;
> Let it; I reck not.
>
> (IX, 171–3)

As is widely agreed, the epic here draws on modes of representation developed on the sixteenth- and seventeenth-century stage. Satan as tragic subject speaks in soliloquies which evoke the utterances of dramatic protagonists like Faustus and Macbeth.

And as in the drama, the themes of the soliloquies in *Paradise Lost* are often the hesitation, uncertainty, doubt and despair of their speakers. After the Fall, Adam, like Hamlet, struggles to grasp the meaning of death. What if only the body dies, leaving the spirit fully conscious? –

> then in the grave,
> Or in some other dismal place who knows
> But I shall die a living death? O thought
> Horrid, if true.
>
> (X, 786–9)

But it cannot *be* true: the spirit and not the body sinned, so both must die together. What, then, if death is not a moment but a process?

> But say
> That death be not one stroke, as I supposed,
> Bereaving sense, but endless misery
> From this day onward
>
> (X, 808–11)

Death is unknown, beyond the consciousness of Adam, who has never witnessed it, and for whom the experience of death may turn out to be precisely the end of consciousness. He cannot work it out alone, and in desperation pushes further and further into the infinite regress of his own subjectivity, only to find there the same absence that Satan too encountered:

O conscience! into what abyss of fears
And horrors hast thou driven me; out of which
I find no way, from deep to deeper plunged.
                              (X, 842-4)

5.2 Plurality

The metaphor is consistently one of depth. In the opposition set
up by humanism what is on display is shallow, superficial;
psychological processes, normally hidden, are profound, and
more profound as they are more thoroughly concealed. *Paradise
Lost* is 'deep' partly to the degree that it human-izes its central
figures, endows them with psychological 'depths'. The metaphor of depth, and the value-judgment inscribed in it, depends,
of course, on the notion of a difference within subjectivity itself,
a difference between what is displayed (action, behaviour) and
what is elsewhere, below the level of the visible (feeling, motive).
For this reason it is not until after the Fall that Adam 'expresses
himself' in soliloquy: innocence knows no difference between
feeling and action, motive and behaviour. Only a figure capable
of error experiences serious doubt, moral uncertainty, inner
conflict, despair. (The soliloquy developed in tragedy, not comedy.) Thus God and the Son appear 'flat' to a humanist reading:
they inhabit no secret inner world of anxiety or anguish.

Satan, on the other hand, dwells in such a world from the
beginning of the poem. From the moment of his opening speech
we know him to be silently racked with deep despair. It is
Satan's soliloquies which carry much of the moral meaning of
the epic, defining the sense of loss, the hopelessness and the
futile malice which make hell intelligible - and unbearable - as
precisely a state of mind, a condition of the subject. At the same
time, of course, it is the soliloquies which elicit the sympathy of
the (humanist) reader, just as Macbeth's solitary utterances,
alternating with displays of further butchery, enlist the audience
in alternating compassion and horror.

The mind of Satan is a richly populated kingdom. In a strategy borrowed and developed from the drama, the soliloquy at
the beginning of Book IV invokes a series of conflicting voices
within a single speech.[1] One of these voices seeks to evade the

despair of the present by constructing imaginary alternatives to
the real position:

> O had his powerful destiny ordained
> Me some inferior angel, I had stood
> Then happy; no unbounded hope had raised
> Ambition.
>
> (IV, 58–61)

'Yet why not?', intervenes a second and more lenient voice (line
61). Another important angel might have raised a revolt and
drawn Satan in. Perhaps there was no real choice. But a third
voice speaks from the position of authority and brooks no
excuse: 'other powers as great/Fell not, but stand unshaken'
(lines 63–4). Satan too could have stood. And the stern voice of
authority addresses him in the second person, and thus from a
place specified as outside the self-indulgence already identified:
'Hadst thou the same free will and power to stand?/Thou hadst'
(lines 66–7). He has therefore no one and nothing to blame but
the divine love itself which gave him free will. The succeeding
voice is petulant: 'Be then his love accursed . . . ' (line 69).
Authority replies, still in the second person: 'Nay cursed be thou
. . . ' (71). The effect of dialogue is sustained as the soliloquy
continues: 'Which way shall I fly?' (line 73); 'Which way I fly is
hell' (line 75). And there follows the account of the self's absolute privation which, for a humanist reader, paradoxically
grounds the soliloquy in the 'reality' (the real absence) which is
the condition of the humanist subject:

>   my self am hell;
> And in the lowest deep a lower deep
> Still threatening to devour me opens wide.
>
> (IV, 75–7)

From the humanist perspective it is at this moment that the
chorus of voices gives way to the real voice of the subject of the
enunciation, the true self which recognizes the truth of its own
condition. This voice, which speaks from the place of the lack,
from the awareness of absence, from the inability to be present
in its own utterance, speaks (the truth) of the un-speakable lower
deep which opens endlessly to devour the subject-speaker. Paradoxically, therefore, these lines only serve precisely to 'deepen'

the effect of a feeling, suffering self made present in the soliloquy, a full identity anterior to speech which knows the condition it speaks of.

The consequence in the Romantic period, when humanism finally cemented its hold, was the emergence of Satan as the tragic hero of the poem. Milton, as Blake famously proclaimed (and examiners diligently reiterate under the rubric 'discuss'), 'was a true poet and of the devil's party without knowing it'.[2] Shelley was filled with admiration for the 'grandeur' of Satan's 'graceful but tremendous spirit' and saw in the account of his inward torture 'the sublimest pathos'.[3] Hazlitt found him 'the most heroic subject that was ever chosen for a poem', and singled out for attention Satan's inner intensity:

> His thoughts burn like a hell within him; but the power of thought holds dominion in his mind over every other consideration. The consciousness of a determined purpose, of 'that intellectual being, those thoughts that wander through eternity', though accompanied with endless pain, he prefers to nonentity . . .[4]

It is often difficult to be sure whether it is Milton's skill or Satan's values which most dazzle these Romantic critics. And here, from a fully humanist perspective, which is after all only a development of the text's own interest in interiority, the plurality of psychological depth becomes apparent. There is every danger that in the course of displaying the nature of hell as a state of mind, the soliloquies may in practice have the effect of destabilizing the moral meaning of the poem. Contempt, malice and despair, the constituents of hell-as-consciousness, become thrilling once they are identified as deep and therefore heroic. The soliloquies of Dr Faustus, to which Satan's speech in Book IV bears a close resemblance, tended to have a similar effect: Faustus too became a Romantic hero.

Paradise Lost apparently recognizes the danger. Unlike the drama, the epic is able to invoke the narrative voice to adjust the view of the reader. Having penetrated the depths of Satan's interiority and found there truth (the truth of the lack), we are then invited by the voice of the text itself to contemplate him from the outside and see his falsehood:

> Thus while he spake, each passion dimmed his face
> Thrice changed with pale, ire, envy and despair,
> Which marred his borrowed visage, and betrayed
> Him counterfeit, if any eye beheld.
>
> (IV, 114–17)

'If any eye beheld.' The illusion is that the reader's does. The body of Satan also speaks, and we see the hypocrisy it betrays. Disguised as a cherub in order to execute his revenge unperceived, Satan, the narrative voice reminds us, is not what he seems. He is inauthentic and, from a humanist standpoint, correspondingly unheroic. Insincerity, the betrayal of the self, is the supreme humanist sin.

Uriel also sees Satan's falsehood:

> whose eye pursued him down
> The way he went, and on the Assyrian mount
> Saw him disfigured, more than could befall
> Spirit of happy sort: his gestures fierce
> He marked and mad demeanour, then alone,
> As he supposed, all unobserved, unseen.
>
> (IV, 125–30)

The angel perceives Satan's condition as madness, beyond the reach of the Law of the Father, outside the symbolic order. But Uriel has not heard the soliloquy. The eye of the reader, however, sees Uriel too. Our gaze, we are to understand, is located beyond these events, outside the fiction itself. The reader shares the comprehensive vision of the omniscient narrator and perceives not only what can be seen (Satan disfigured and apparently mad), but also what is invisible except to God (Satan's real state of mind). The narrative voice offers to share its omniscience with us so that we are able to see and judge Satan from the point of view of God. (If the Romantics failed to take full moral advantage of this invitation, that is partly because they had already turned their backs on an antihumanist deity.)

Drama has no place for the narrative voice which offers to discipline the gaze of the reader by aligning it with God's. (Classic realist drama of the nineteenth and twenthieth centuries supplies this deficiency by elaborate stage directions which ensure that the audience is shown a truth against which to measure the utterances of the characters.) In *Samson Agonistes* the Chorus performs some of the functions of the narrative voice. The Chorus tells important parts of the story: it describes Samson's outward appearance (lines 118–23) (betraying, perhaps, that this is a text for reading rather than performance); it narrates his past history (lines 128–50); and it introduces and describes the characters to the blind Samson and the unknowing spectator or reader:

> But see here comes thy reverend sire
> With careful steps, locks white as down,
> Old Manoa.
>
> (326–8)

Samson Agonistes is a drama of interiority. It records the processes of temptation and despair, the inward intervention of divine grace, Samson's consequent submission to the will of God and the return of his heroic powers as a result. At the beginning of the play Samson is isolated by his blindness from contact with the external world. The outward objects of his gaze 'annulled' (line 72), he retreats into his own subjectivity, where he finds nothing but restless thoughts that rush upon him 'like a deadly swarm/Of hornets armed' (lines 19–20). Every newcomer awakens another inward grief (line 330). Despairing because he has failed to fulfil the promise of a special destiny, a life 'separate to God' (line 31), Samson describes himself as worse than dead, in a metaphor which resembles Satan's impossible 'lower deep':

> but O yet more miserable!
> Myself, my sepulchre, a moving grave,
> Buried, yet not exempt
> By privilege of death and burial
> From worst of other evils, pains and wrongs.
>
> (101–5)

At last, having struggled in vain to make sense of his own condition, Samson feels 'Some rousing motions' in him (1382). In obedience to this divine imperative he agrees to attend the Philistines in their temple. From then on the story is recounted by a Messenger, who relates how Samson pulls down the pillars of the temple, destroying himself and his captors among the ruins of their own festival.

The problems of *Samson Agonistes* is that the ethics of the play are extraordinarily bloodthirsty. The story ends with all the subtlety of the last reel of a Western. The effect of the divine imperative is violence, destruction and lamentation. Manoa assures us that this is a fitting end to Samson's heroic life (lines 1079–11), that God was with his champion to the end (lines 1719–20), and that there is no cause for tears: 'nothing but well and fair,/And what may quiet us in a death so noble' (lines 1723–4). But it is hard, since the issue is not debated in the text, to quell a lingering anxiety about whether Samson's action is not perhaps rather in excess of justice. After all, he himself betrayed his secret to Dalila. The political implications for the Jews of his final act merit only an equivocal allusion:

> To Israel
> Honour hath left, and freedom, let but them
> Find courage to lay hold on this occasion.
> (1714–16)

The main proposition seems to be that God defends his elect by procuring the most violent revenge for injuries which are the direct consequence of their own actions.

The Chorus offers reassurance:

> All is best, though we oft doubt,
> What the unsearchable dispose
> Of highest wisdom brings about.
> (1745–7)

This is apparently an allusion to the relationship between Samson's own uncertainty and the providential control which continues to work in defiance of human blindness. But despite its tendency to magisterial pronouncements (especially on the nature of women), the Chorus never possesses the authority of an omniscient narrator. It consists of Samson's 'friends and neighbours' (line 180), and they are inclined to speak with the voice of common sense, which is by no means the same thing as omniscience. They do not know everything – what Harapha has come for (lines 1070, 1075) or what will become of Samson in the Philistine temple (line 1380). Consequently it is possible to detect in their comments on the nature of the divine wisdom, an entirely human, if unconscious, acknowledgment that 'unsearchable' Providence does not make very much sense to ordinary people. If so, while the narrative voice in *Paradise Lost* offers the reader the position of God, in order to contain and discipline our judgment of the characters, the Chorus in *Samson Agonistes*, not necessarily any more knowing than the protagonist himself, merely reiterates the ethical doubts of the human reader. The uncertainty engendered by the ending is not dispelled.

It makes all the difference. *Samson Agonistes* can be read either as a closed affirmation of Christian Providence, or as an interogative text which calls in question the benevolence of 'highest wisdom'. The moral dangers of such plurality are at once apparent. In a world of warring sects and incipient atheism the ethical project of Milton's future writing evidently necessitates the firm discipline of an omniscient narrative voice.

5.3 Towards the novel

Interiority as the motive force and explanation of action, the story of a special, marginal individual, and a narrative voice which proclaims the truth of the fiction: these features of Milton's final poem all point in the direction of the novel. *Samson Agonistes* remains a drama, without a single, clearly authorized voice to fix its meaning; despite its attention to subjectivity-as-destiny, *Paradise Lost* in its breadth of focus and its claims to universality is still palpably an epic; but the narrative strategies of *Paradise Regained* begin to bear a clearer resemblance to those of the emergent novel. More evidently than *Paradise Lost*, *Paradise Regained* anticipates the classic realist text.[5]

Classic realist fiction is characteristically specific in its focus. The nineteenth-century novel and its modern derivatives (or, for that matter, Hollywood film or television soap opera) tell the story of one individual, one family or a single community, and however representative these may seem to be, the strategies of the text set out to produce an effect of specificity. *Paradise Lost* knows no such boundaries. It is the story of '*man's* first disobedience', which is the source of '*all* our woe', and its project is 'to justify the ways of God' in general 'to men' in general. Its

setting is the entire cosmos and its chronological range eternity.
If the opening lines of *Paradise Lost* also allude to '*one* greater
man', that is simply an acknowledgement that history cannot be
made without specific and identified protagonists. The opening
of *Paradise Regained*, by contrast, reverses the emphasis. Here it is
the individual protagonists who occupy the foreground (even at
the cost of the explicit elimination of Eve), though the text concedes that their actions have implications for us all:

> I who erewhile the happy garden sung,
> By one man's disobedience lost, now sing
> Recovered Paradise to all mankind,
> By one man's firm obedience fully tried
> Through all temptation, and the tempter foiled
> In all his wiles, defeated and repulsed.
>
>   (I, 1–6)

As the story begins, a figure emerges from the crowd to be
baptized. He is believed to be the son of Joseph (line 23) and he
is 'obscure,/Unmarked, unknown' (lines 24–5). Almost at once,
however, he is identified as special, when the dove descends and
God's voice pronounces him his Son (line 32). The text is the
story of this individual, at once ordinary and set apart, both
representative and privileged, in his struggle against a single
enemy who is sophisticated, wily, plausible and a master of
disguise. If the conflict between two such adversaries has its
roots in romance, and a direct parallel in the Red Cross
Knight's encounter with Archimago, it also points forward to
classic realist fiction and to the contest between Tom Jones and
Blifil, Holmes and Moriarty, or Sam Spade and the Fat Man.

Christ's first words in the poem are a long soliloquy concerning his identity. The difference within his subjectivity (he is both
man and God) releases the uncertainty which motivates the
utterance. The project is partly, of course, to provide the reader
with information about Christ's childhood, but the narrative
device, the frame within which the information is contained, is
introspection. Similarly, Andrew and Simon express their per-
plexity at Christ's disappearance and their sense nevertheless of
his providential destiny in a (joint) soliloquy (II, 30–57); and
this is closely followed by the musings of Mary, who meditates in
solitude on his absence and its meaning.

The effect is to foreground interiority and to lay stress on individual psychology as the material of narrative. Something of the difference between this text and *Paradise Lost* can be seen in a new use of the epic simile. I have suggested that the Vallombrosa comparison reveals relatively little about the condition of the fallen angels who are at its starting-point, but constitutes instead a demonstration of the ways of divine justice and divine Providence throughout history (see pp. 37–8 above). In contrast, the following multiple simile from *Paradise Regained* analyses primarily the nature of the two individuals concerned: it illumi-nates the motivation of Satan and the identity of Christ. Satan has failed to secure a victory by offering the kingdoms of the world, and for a moment he hesitates:

> But as a man who had been matchless held
> In cunning, over-reached where least he thought,
> To salve his credit, and for very spite
> Still will be tempting him who foils him still,
> And never cease, though to his shame the more;
> Or as a swarm of flies in vintage-time,
> About the wine-press where sweet must is poured,
> Beat off, returns as oft with humming sound;
> Or surging waves against a solid rock,
> Though all to shivers dashed, the assault renew,
> Vain battery, and in froth or bubbles end;
> So Satan, whom repulse upon repulse
> Met ever; and to shameful silence brought,
> Yet gives not o'er though desperate of success,
> And his vain importunity pursues.
>
> (IV, 10–24)

The simile is no less textual than the Vallombrosa instance: there is a parallel for the flies in Homer and another in Ariosto; the rock and the waves have analogues in Homer and Virgil. But this time the effect is not to show the constancy of God's ways at different times and in different places. On the contrary, the main project seems to be to establish the plausibility, the *naturalness* of Satan's persistence even when the case is patently hopeless: debating champions, flies and waves all similarly refuse to acknowledge defeat. Christ, meanwhile, is identified as a greater champion, like a rock, impregnable. The multiple simile throws into relief the specific relationship between the two adversaries, and if there are more general implications (the wine-press is eucharistic, the rock is the foundation of the Christian faith), these are available at an additional and secondary level of interpretation.

Paradise Lost is only tentatively interested in *vraisemblance*, the accumulation of detail which constructs the illusion of a 'real' context and setting for the events of the story. The novel becomes increasingly conscious of *vraisemblance* as it becomes increasingly illusionist in its strategies: clothes, architecture, menus and modes of transport are all specified in nineteenth-century fiction in order to deepen the illusion of reality. Modern classic realist novelists 'research' the settings of their work, in quest of the accuracy which guarantees plausibility. *Paradise Lost* pays some attention to the visual delights of Eden and the digestive habits of the angels, and the account of Adam sitting in the doorway of the bower, while Eve gets their vegetarian lunch, carries considerable patriarchal conviction (V, 299–307). There are also moments when Adam and Eve appear engagingly idiosyncratic (see pp. 60–1 above). But on the whole the specific details of heaven and hell are not important in the epic, and historical accuracy is not, of course, much of an issue.

In *Paradise Regained*, however, historical verisimilitude is sustained in some detail. Tiberius is currently Emperor of Rome (III, 159), but Julius Caesar, 'whom now all the world admires', is not forgotten (III, 39). The moment of the temptation is thus clearly specified. When historical figures are invoked in the discussion, they date from the period before Christ. In the debate on knowledge the texts concerned could all have been known to the historical Jesus. As the allusions become slightly esoteric from the Jewish perspective, Christ himself offers an explanation: 'for throughout the world/To me is not unknown what hath been done/Worthy of memorial' (II, 443–5). From the high mountain Jesus can see the Parthians preparing to attack the Scythians; and in a delightful detail, Satan points out the embassies in foreign clothes making for Rome along the Appian Way. The construction of reality is evidently part of the project of *Paradise Regained*.

Classic realism depends on the introduction of an enigma, which generates suspense, and leads ultimately to a disclosure, that is also the resolution of the story. In *Paradise Regained* the enigma seems to be Christ's identity. Who is he? Is he right in thinking he is the Son of God? What are the limits of his resistance to temptation? Are there any constraints on his power? Of course, the suspense is radically reduced by the familiarity of the biblical story, but the text constructs moments of uncertainty which have no scriptural origin. The aged man in rural weeds is not identified until after he has explained how beneficial to the local poor it would be if Christ were to turn the stones into bread. There are few digressions to delay the unfolding of the story. On the contrary, suspense is intensified by a feeling of haste. Satan, putting forward his plan in hell, stresses the urgency of the threat: 'Ye see our danger on the utmost edge/Of hazard' (I, 94–5). And the narrative confirms what he says: 'no time was then/For long indulgence to their fears or grief' (I, 109–10). However long the debates between Satan and Christ may seem to the modern reader, evidently *Paradise Regained* is not an appropriate place for the protracted excursions and baroque textuality of the earlier epic.

The enigma is not permitted, however, to generate radical uncertainty, since the narrative voice is always there to contain real doubt. Satan's arguments constitute a test for the reader. Could he be right about the value of pagan knowledge or the use of miracles to feed the poor? Doesn't even the Devil deserve forgiveness? But the poem effortlessly directs the reader's judgement: 'To whom our Saviour sternly thus replied . . .' (I, 406). The control is consistently evident in the adverbs: 'To whom thus Jesus temperately . . .' (II, 378); 'To whom thus Jesus patiently . . .' (II, 432).

The moment of disclosure finally specifies the whole truth of the relationship between hero and villain. Challenged to reveal his identity, Christ stands on the pinnacle:

Tempt not the Lord thy God, he said and stood.
But Satan smitten with amazement fell.
(IV, 561–2)

This instant of perfect symmetry between the adversaries makes intelligible all that has gone before, drawing on and holding together in a single retrospect the meanings of standing and falling throughout both epics: ˋ

> Ingrate, he had of me
> All he could have; I made him just and right,
> Sufficient to have stood, though free to fall.
> Such I created all the ethereal powers
> And spirits, both them who stood and them who failed;
> Freely they stood who stood, and fell who fell.
>
> *(Paradise Lost*, III, 97–102)

> from morn
> To noon he fell, from noon to dewy eve.
>
> *(Paradise Lost*, I, 742–3)

> Nine days they fell; confounded Chaos roared,
> And felt tenfold confusion in their fall
> Through his wild anarchy, so huge a rout
> Encumbered him with ruin: hell at last
> Yawning received them whole, and on them closed.
>
> *(Paradise Lost*, VI, 871–5)

> firm they might have stood,
> Yet fell; remember, and fear to transgress.
>
> *(Paradise Lost*, VI, 911–12)

> stand fast; to stand or fall
> Free in thine own arbitrament it lies.
>
> *(Paradise Lost*, VIII, 640–1)

> fall down,
> And worship me as thy superior lord.
>
> *(Paradise Regained*, IV, 166–7)

> ill wast thou shrouded then,
> O patient Son of God, yet only stood'st
> Unshaken.
>
> *(Paradise Regained*, IV, 419–21)

The fall of Satan from the pinnacle re-enacts the fall of the angels and restores Satan to his proper habitation. The choice Christ is offered reiterates the choice offered to Adam and Eve. And the choice Christ makes repairs the damage of their Fall and regains salvation. The moment thus signifies beyond itself, specifies and fixes the meanings of good and evil, the Fall and Christ's redemption. The narrative voice authoritatively discloses the truth and closes the story, placing the reader in a position to share its authority, its mastery, its omniscience.

Or does it?

5.4 The return of the repressed

Does the narrative voice escape the problem of differance?

The project of classic realist narrative is to repress its own textuality, constructing the illusion of a knowledge which is inter-subjectively shared by narrator and reader, and which transcends the text itself. The aim is to overcome the plurality that is an effect of differance, offering the reader an imaginary truth which is stable and non-contradictory, because it exists outside the instability and undecidability of language. Knowledge is thus invisibly transmitted from the knowing author to a reader capable of apprehending it. When the narrative voice is authorized by God, the truth it has to impart, though theoretically open to everyone, is probably in practice fully available only to warfaring Christians, those who are already 'sufficient both to judge aright and to examine each matter'.

In other words, the classic realist theory of communication is based not on the diligence or the linguistic competence of the reader, but on some much more mysterious quality, a metaphysical 'sufficiency' which the reader already shares with the narrator. This is the ground on which Christ rejects pagan knowledge in *Paradise Regained*. Satan promises him learning which will render him an autonomous subject, omnipotent within himself (IV, 283–4). Christ, who predictably turns out to be capable already of analysing the shortcomings of all branches of pagan knowledge, nevertheless replies 'sagely' (line 285) that such learning is trivial or worse. Not only is it all inferior, both morally and poetically, to the Scriptures; more important, true wisdom comes from somewhere else, not from what is written but from a direct encounter with the only origin of truth: 'he who receives/Light from above, from the fountain of light,/No other doctrine needs' (lines 288–90). And this extra-textual

'light' is in turn the origin of the reader's extra-linguistic sufficiency. Reading is unprofitable unless the reader brings to it 'A
spirit and judgment equal or superior' to the work itself and,
culminating argument, 'what he brings, what needs he elsewhere seek?' (lines 324–5).

It is ironic that this repudiation of textuality occurs in a poem
steeped morally and poetically not only in the Scriptures but also
in the pagan epic and georgic traditions. And Christ is in a
position to specify in a series of aphorisms the inadequacies of
the pagan philosophers, for the benefit of the Christian reader,
precisely because he has read them (IV, 293ff) Textuality is not
so easily repressed.

Nor does the moment of disclosure on the pinnacle escape the
constraints of textuality, and this time it is the textuality of
Scripture itself which is at issue. 'To whom thus Jesus: Also it is
written,/Tempt not the Lord thy God' (IV, 560–1). *Paradise
Regained* here quotes the New Testament, which in turn quotes
the Old Testament (Matthew iv, 7; Luke iv, 12; Deuteronomy
vi, 16), and each reinscription produces a difference which,
however marginally, problematizes its meaning.

In *Paradise Regained* the problem is finally undecidable.
Beyond the enigma of Christ's identity the text raises a more
serious and altogether more linguistic question, which it never
resolves: what is the *meaning* of Christ's identity? Of course, a
good many contributions to the answer are offered – in the
images and in the adverbs, for instance. Christ is a wine-press, a
rock; he is stern, temperate, patient, sage. But the problem is
more complex than that. Satan grasps it. He tells Christ that he
wants to uncover a single meaning for the profoundly plural
proclamation at his baptism, to find out

> In what degree or meaning thou art called
> The Son of God, which bears no single sense;
> The Son of God I also am, or was,
> And if I was, I am; relation stands;
> All men are Sons of God; yet thee I thought
> In some respect far higher so declared.
>
> (IV, 516–21)

In what special sense, if any, is Jesus the Son of God?

Satan is asking the meaning of the Incarnation. What single

relationship between human and divine differentiates Christ from angels, from other human beings and from God? It matters to Satan because the Incarnation spells his imminent defeat. And in the economy of the poem it matters to the reader. To what extent is Christ human, a model, a true warfaring Christian, able to be emulated? To what extent is he divine, able to bring about the Atonement?

The episode on the pinnacle – human audacity or superhuman miracle – does not resolve that question. Nor does Christ's utterance: 'Tempt not the Lord thy God'. What exactly is it that the event discloses? That Christ is God and can stand, can stand because he is God, and that Satan should recognize defeat and stop tempting him? Or that Christ as human being should risk the consequences of standing, rather than put God to the test of performing a miracle to save him? The elusive – that is the dispersed, disseminated, because differed and deferred – meaning of the utterance depends precisely on its textuality.

'It is written.' The Devil himself has just quoted Scripture, inviting Christ, if not to stand, to cast himself down, relying on divine intervention:

> safely if Son of God:
> For it is written, He will give command
> Concerning thee to his angels, in their hands
> They shall uplift thee.
>   (IV, 555–8; cf. Psalm xci, 11–12)

Christ turns the Scriptures back against him, quoting Moses: 'Ye shall not tempt the Lord your God, as ye tempted him in Massah' (Deutronomy vi, 16). In this context the utterance remains cryptic, but the allusion to Massah (which means temptation) refers back to an episode described in the book of Exodus (xvii, 1–7). At the end of forty years in the wilderness the Jews pitched camp and found that there was no water for them to drink. They complained against Moses and doubted whether God was truly with them. On God's instructions Moses struck water from the rock, reproaching the people none the less for 'tempting' (challenging) God. The water was commonly understood in the Middle Ages and the Renaissance as a type or foreshadowing of the life-giving eucharistic blood, struck by the soldier from the side of Christ on the cross.[6]

After forty years in the wilderness the Children of Israel put God to the test. After forty days in the wilderness does the Son of God refuse to repeat their error? If so, does he show himself human, a true warfaring Christian, or divine and a source of life-giving water in the desert? The ambiguity depends on the accumulated meanings of the quotations he utters.

The New Testament accounts of the episode on the pinnacle make no reference to standing or falling. In *Paradise Regained* this crucial difference deepens the undecidability of the episode's meaning, and again the uncertainty is specifically textual. Satan falls, as he fell before, but Christ stands, the second Adam, reversing the Fall which brought death into the world, and all our woe. In the poem this moment then becomes the turning-point of the divine comedy. But the authority of the narrative voice does nothing to diminish the undecidability. As the second Adam, is Christ man? Or God?

He is, of course, the Son of God. The indeterminacy is precisely the Christian project. The mystery of the Incarnation is that Christ *is* God *and* other than God, 'True image of the Father', 'with godlike force endued' (IV, 596, 602), human, a model, able to be emulated. The meaning of the Incarnation is undecidable.[7] But there is no meaning, and in consequence no undecidability, without language.

A text has no meaning outside textuality. The account of the episode on the pinnacle displays something of the nature of textual meaning. Any word, any utterance, is intelligible to the degree that it is a reiteration, always alluding to other utterances, always already 'written', but always and inevitably differing from what has gone before. Meaning is an effect of difference because it is the product of a long vista back through all the other invocations of the meanings from which it differs.

It is for this reason that meaning is for us now no longer a metaphysical mystery, like Milton's Incarnation, but a site of struggle, a place to lay claim to the possibilities we want to realize. As in Milton's texts, gender and sovereignty, and even, in their own way, poetry and narrative, are all still caught up in contests for meaning. In place of the fixity of eternal truth, differance and dissemination mobilize meaning, identify it as the location of a process of change in which we are all able to take part, since meanings are produced and not given.

And Milton's final poem reverts to the concerns that dominated 'The Nativity Ode' of forty years earlier: the Incarnation-
as-signifier and the textuality of meaning. These can in a sense
be regarded as the same concern, namely, the question of differance. All Milton's writing engages with this issue in one way or
another; and all of it can be read, sometimes in spite of itself, as
celebrating the possibilities released by an encounter with a process of production that cannot be arrested.

Notes

Chapter 1 Turning-points

1   All references to Milton's poetry are to *The Poems of John Milton*, ed. John Carey and Alastair Fowler (London: Longmans, 1968). Quotations are from this edition. I have reproduced the dates of composition given by Carey and Fowler.

2   The standard biography is W. R. Parker, *Milton* (2 vols, Oxford: Clarendon Press, 1968).

3   Jacques Derrida, 'Différance', in *Margins of Philosophy*, trans. Alan Bass (Brighton: Harvester, 1982), pp. 1–27. Much of Derrida's theory of language is available in relatively accessible form in three interviews he gave between 1967 and 1971; see *Positions*, trans. Alan Bass (London: Athlone Press, 1987).

4   Derrida, *Positions*, p. 20.

5   The work of Christopher Hill is indispensable to any analysis of the history of this period: see especially *The Century of Revolution 1603–1714* (London: Nelson, 1961), and *Reformation to Industrial Revolution: a Social and Economic History of Britain 1530–1780* (London: Weidenfeld and Nicolson, 1967). For an overview of the Tudor and Stuart pretensions to absolutism see Perry Anderson, *Lineages of the Absolutist State* (London: NLB, 1974), pp. 113–42. Brian Manning analyses the politics of the Civil War in *The English People and the English Revolution* (London: Penguin, 1978). For the theoretical debate about the meaning of the Revolution see Paul Sweezy et al., *The Transition from Feudalism to Capitalism* (London: NLB, 1976).

6   Derek Hirst, *Authority and Conflict: England 1603–1658* (London: Edward Arnold, 1986), p. 9. For a discussion of the significance of coffee houses as places where bourgeois civil society was produced and reproduced, see Peter Stallybrass and Allon White, *The Politics and Poetics of Transgression* (London: Methuen, 1986), pp. 94–100.

7   Mark Girouard traces many of these changes in *Life in the English Country House* (London: Penguin, 1980), pp. 119–62.

8   Christopher Hill, *Milton and the English Revolution* (London: Faber, 1977). See also Andrew Milner, *John Milton and the English Revolution: a Study in the Sociology of Literature* (London: Macmillan, 1981).

9   Fredric Jameson reads *Paradise Lost* as marking a turning-point between feudalism and capitalism. Satan's revolt is baronial, but Adam is the first bourgeois, destined at that moment to inherit the earth. See 'Religion and Ideology: a Political Reading of *Paradise Lost*', in *Literature, Politics and Theory*, ed. Francis Barker et al. (London: Methuen, 1986), pp. 35–56.

10 For consistency I have continued to reproduce the dates given by Carey and Fowler. In this instance their position seems to me slightly eccentric: *Samson Agonistes* is conventionally dated late in the 1660s. But since the date is not important to my argument, I have not joined in the debate.

11 All references to Milton's prose are to the *Complete Prose Works of John Milton*, ed. Don M. Wolfe (8 vols, New Haven: Yale University Press, 1953–82).

Chapter 2 Poetry

1   I have modernized the spelling and typography of the prose works.

2   Jacques Derrida, 'Différance', in *Margins of Philosophy*, trans. Alan Bass (Brighton: Harvester, 1982), p. 20.

3   I have modernized the punctuation of this poem for the sake of the syntax.

4   See chapter 3, n. 5 below.

5   F. R. Leavis, 'Milton's Verse' (1933), in *Revaluation: Tradition and Development in English Poetry* (London: Penguin, 1964), pp. 42–61, see pp. 46–7.

6   John Hollander, *The Untuning of the Sky* (Princeton: Princeton University Press, 1961), pp. 163–73.

7   Antony Easthope, *Poetry as Discourse* (London: Methuen, 1983), pp. 69–77.

8   Antony Easthope, 'Towards the Autonomous Subject in Poetry: Milton's "On his Blindness"', in *Post-structuralist Readings of English Poetry*, ed. Richard Machin and Christopher Norris (Cambridge: Cambridge University Press, 1987), pp. 122–33, see pp. 128–9.

9   F. T. Prince, *The Italian Element in Milton's Verse* (Oxford: Clarendon Press, 1954), pp. 84–8.

10 Samuel Johnson, *Lives of the English Poets*, ed. George Birkbeck Hill (3 vols, Oxford: Clarendon Press, 1905), vol. 1, p. 90.

11 *The Poems of John Milton*, ed. John Carey and Alastair Fowler (London: Longmans, 1968), p. 430.

12 Leavis, 'Milton's Verse', p. 50.

13 Christopher Ricks, *Milton's Grand Style* (Oxford: Clarendon Press, 1963), p. 38.

14 Carey and Fowler (eds), *The Poems of John Milton*, p. 433.

15 R. D. Emma, *Milton's Grammar* (The Hague: Mouton, 1964), pp. 27, 122, 139.

16   Johnson, *Lives*, vol. 1, pp. 190–1.
17   Geoffrey Hartman, 'Milton's Counterplot', in *Beyond Formalism* (New Haven: Yale University Press, 1970), pp. 113–23.
18   Fredric Jameson, *Fables of Aggression* (Berkeley: University of California Press, 1979), p. 76.
19   Hartman, 'Counterplot', p. 118.
20   T. S. Eliot, 'Milton', *Proceedings of the British Academy* 33 (1947), 74–5.
21   James Whaler, 'The Miltonic Simile', *PMLA* 46 (1931), pp. 1034–74, see p. 1050.
22   Leavis, 'Milton's Verse', pp. 57–8.
23   John Hollander, *The Figure of Echo: a Mode of Allusion in Milton and After* (Berkeley: University of California Press, 1981), pp. 38–41.
24   Ibid., p. 41.
25   Ricks, *Grand Style*, p. 65.
26   John Hollander, *Vision and Resonance: Two Senses of Poetic Form* (New York: Oxford University Press, 1975), p. 95.
27   Cf. Colin MacCabe, who points out that Ricks's powerful defence of Milton's 'grand style' stays within the framework of Leavis's original attack (Milton's style is/is not expressive), and therefore ignores the more interesting point made by T. S. Eliot in his British Academy lecture, that Milton's style reminds him of Joyce and Mallarmé. (Colin MacCabe, ' "So Truth be in the Field"': Milton's Use of Language', in *Teaching the Text*, ed. Susanne Kappeler and Norman Bryson (London: Routledge and Kegan Paul, 1983), pp. 18–34.) It would be worth considering, however, whether what Joyce and Mallarmé make is meaning(s) or non-sense. The anarchist group Tel Quel would have argued in favour of the latter as a form of liberation. That is not the point I am making about Milton.

Chapter 3 Gender

1   For a detailed account of this uncertainty see Catherine Belsey, *The Subject of Tragedy: Identity and Difference in Renaissance Drama* (London: Methuen, 1985), pp. 149–221.
2   Richard Brathwait, *The English Gentlewoman* (London, 1631), pp. 89–90.
3   For a helpful account of the conventions of the masque see John G. Demaray, *Milton and the Masque Tradition: the Early Poems, 'Arcades' and Comus* (Cambridge, Mass.: Harvard University Press, 1968); Stephen Orgel, *The Illusion of Power: Political Theater in the English Renaissance* (Berkeley: University of California Press, 1975), see especially chapter 2.
4   For a discussion of the political meaning and context of *Comus* see Cedric C. Brown, *John Milton's Aristocratic Entertainments* (Cambridge: Cambridge University Press, 1985), especially chapter 3.
5   E. M. W. Tillyard calls this Comus's 'great speech', in the tradition of the Church Fathers, though he concedes that Comus 'overdoes it' towards the end (Tillyard, *Studies in Milton* (London: Chatto and Windus, 1951), p. 89). Kenneth Muir held that neither Comus nor the Lady was right, though the poetry implied support for Comus ('300 years

of Milton's Poems', *Penguin New Writing* 24 (1945), 128–46, see p. 142). David Wilkinson finds the Lady insecure and unpersuasive, and 'the potent speech of Comus unresolved' ('The Escape from Pollution: a Comment on *Comus*', *Essays in Criticism* 10 (1960), 32–43, see p. 39). It is not clear whether it is the Lady's economics or her sexual politics that these critics find so uncongenial.

6   Ovid, *Metamorphoses I–IV*, ed. and tr. D.E. Hill (Warminster and Oak Park, Illinois: Aris and Phillips and Bolchazy-Carducci, 1985). pp. 182–3.

7   See for example Bathsua Makin, *An Essay to Revive the Ancient Education of Gentlewomen* (London, 1673); Mary Astell, *Some Reflections Upon Marriage*, in *The First English Feminist*, ed. Bridget Hill (Aldershot: Gower, 1986). As late as 1925, however, Freud was still reaffirming the stereotype, unconsciously motivated, at least if we read in accordance with his own theories, by the threat from contemporary feminism, which makes a sudden and otherwise 'unnecessary' appearance at the end of an essay on penis-envy:

> I cannot evade the notion (though I hesitate to give it expression) that for women the level of what is ethically normal is different from what it is in men. Their super-ego is never so inexorable, so impersonal, so independent of its emotional origins as we require it to be in men. Character-traits which critics of every epoch have brought up against women – that they show less sense of justice than men, that they are less ready to submit to the great exigencies of life, that they are more often influenced in their judgements by feelings of affection or hostility – all these would be amply accounted for by the modification in the formation of their super-ego which we have inferred above. We must not allow ourselves to be deflected from such conclusions by the denials of the feminists . . .

Sigmund Freud, 'Some Psychical Consequences of the the Anatomical Distinction Between the Sexes', in *On Sexuality*, The Pelican Freud Library, (London: Penguin, 1977), vol. 7, pp. 323–43, see p. 342.

8   Milton, *The Doctrine and Discipline of Divorce*, in *Complete Prose Works of John Milton*, ed. Don M. Wolfe (8 vols, New Haven, Yale University Press, 1953–82) vol. 2, p. 465.

9   Robert Graves, *Wife to Mr Milton* (London: Penguin, 1954).

10   Cf. IV, 635–8.

11   Sandra M. Gilbert and Susan Gubar, *The Madwoman in the Attic: the Woman Writer and the Nineteenth-Century Literary Imagination* (New Haven: Yale University Press, 1979). On *Shirley*, see pp. 193–5.

12   See for example Christine Froula, 'When Eve Reads Milton: Undoing the Canonical Economy', *Critical Inquiry* 10 (1983–4), 321–37. Note 12 of this essay lists some previous discussions of Milton's sexual politics (p. 345). Mary Nyquist, 'The Father's Word/Satan's Wrath', *PMLA* 100 (1985), 187–202, takes feminism for granted in the reading, though it is not a central issue. Mary Nyquist also locates Milton's work within a

feminist reading of history: 'Fallen Differences, Phallogocentric Discourses: Losing *Paradise Lost* to History', in *Post-structuralism and the Question of History*, ed. Derek Attridge, Geoff Bennington and Robert Young (Cambridge: Cambridge University Press, 1987), pp. 212–43; and 'The Genesis of Gendered Subjectivity in the Divorce Tracts and in *Paradise Lost*', in *Re-membering Milton: Essays on the Texts and Traditions*, ed. Mary Nyquist and Margaret W. Ferguson (New York: Methuen, forthcoming).

13   Shoshana Felman, 'Turning the Screw of Interpretation', in *Literature and Psychoanalysis: the Question of Reading: Otherwise*, ed. Shoshana Felman (Baltimore: Johns Hopkins University Press, 1982), pp. 94–207. See also Barbara Johnson, 'The Frame of Reference: Poe, Lacan, Derrida', in ibid., pp. 457–505.

14   Cf. Mary Nyquist, 'Reading the Fall: Discourse and Drama in *Paradise Lost*', *ELR* 14 (1984), 199–229.

15   Robert Graves, 'The Ghost of Milton', in *The Crowning Privilege: Collected Essays on Poetry* (London: Penguin, 1959), pp. 331–43, see especially pp. 334, 338–9, 342–3.

16   See for example Philip Stubbes, *The Anatomy of Abuses* (London, 1583), sig. F ii–iii, G iii–iv; William Prynne, *Histrio-Mastix*, (London, 1633), pp. 184ff.

Chapter 4 Sovereignty

1   'The imaginary' and 'the symbolic order' are terms from Lacanian psychoanalysis. In what follows I draw on Lacan's account of desire. The best exposition of Lacan I know is Arthur W. Frank's hitherto unpublished *Reading Pornography: Self-Production in Popular Culture*. Jane Gallop, *Reading Lacan* (Ithaca: Cornell University Press, 1985), is excellent but is not addressed to beginners. For an introduction to Lacanian theory see Malcolm Bowie, 'Jacques Lacan', in *Structuralism and Since: From Lévi-Strauss to Derrida*, ed. John Sturrock (Oxford: Oxford University Press, 1979), pp. 116–53.

2   Milton, *Christian Doctrine*, pp. 203–80.

3   Jacques Lacan, *Ecrits*, trans. Alan Sheridan (London: Tavistock, 1977), pp. 263, 264.

4   Cf. Antony Easthope, 'The Politicization of English', *PN Review* 40 (1984), 4.

5   Arthur O. Lovejoy, 'Milton and the Paradox of the Fortunate Fall', in *Milton's Epic Poetry*, ed. C. A. Patrides (London: Penguin, 1967), pp. 55–73.

6   For a sceptical account of master-narratives as knowledge and as power see Jean-François Lyotard, *The Postmodern Condition: a Report on Knowledge*, trans. Geoff Bennington and Brian Massumi (Manchester: Manchester University Press, 1984).

Chapter 5 Narrative

1 For a discussion of this strategy in the drama see Catherine Belsey, *The Subject of Tragedy: Identity and Difference in Renaissance Drama* (London: Methuen, 1985), pp. 44–51.

2 William Blake, *The Marriage of Heaven and Hell, Complete Writings*, ed. Geoffrey Keynes (London: Oxford University Press, 1966), p. 150.

3 P. B. Shelley, 'On the Devil, and Devils', in *Shelley's Prose*, ed. David Lee Clark (Albuquerque: University of New Mexico Press, 1966), pp. 268, 270.

4 William Hazlitt, 'On Shakespeare and Milton', in *The Collected Works*, ed. A. R. Waller and Arnold Glover (12 vols, London: Dent, 1902), vol. 5, pp. 63–4.

5 For a discussion of the characteristic features of classic realism see Catherine Belsey, *Critical Practice* (London: Methuen, 1980), pp. 67–84.

6 Cf. Milton, *Christian Doctrine*, p. 554.

7 *Christian Doctrine* stresses the profound mystery of the Incarnation (pp. 420–9), and argues that 'it is best for us to be ignorant of things which God wishes to remain secret' (p. 424). Christ incarnate is emphatically both man and God in this text.

Index

history 5, 8, 10–15, 18, 38, 86, 96, 97
Hollander, John 42–3, 107, 108
humanism, humanist 9, 13, 14, 16–18, 30, 35–6, 45, 60–1, 62, 64, 77, 81, 82–3, 85–92

imaginary 14, 22, 68, 70, 73, 75, 101, 110
imperialism 13, 35–6
interiority 60, 76, 83, 85–95, 97
interpretation 6–7, 9, 21, 26

Jameson, Fredric 107, 108
Johnson, Barbara 110
Johnson, Samuel 34, 35, 107, 108
Jones, Inigo 47
Jonson, Ben 47, 48

Lacan, Jacques 33–4, 70–1, 110
lack 34, 60, 68, 70, 75, 76, 90, 91
Leavis, F.R. 34, 38, 107, 108
logocentrism 45
Logos 20, 23, 24, 26, 36, 39, 41, 43, 50
Lovejoy, Arthur O. 82, 110
Lycidas 8, 16, 28–34, 63, 65–6
Lyotard, Jean-François 110

MacCabe, Colin 108
Makin, Bathsua 109
'man' 15–17, 35, 95–6, 104
Man with a Movie Camera 24
Manning, Brian 106
marriage 14, 54–6, 61
meaning 10, 13, 14, 20, 21, 26, 38, 39, 41, 42, 44–5, 50, 70, 75, 101, 104
 and difference 6–7, 21, 23, 68–70, 74
 and power 8–9
 and presence 6–7, 19–20, 23–4
 and textuality 18, 102–5
 indeterminacy (undecidability) of 42, 43, 63, 104
metaphysical, metaphysics 6–7, 18, 45, 76, 84, 101, 104
'Methought I saw my late espoused saint' (Sonnet XIX) 55

Milner, Andrew 107
Muir, Kenneth 108–9

Nyquist, Mary 109–10

'Ode on the Morning of Christ's Nativity' ('The Nativity Ode') 1–5, 15, 17, 19–23, 24, 26, 30, 31, 40, 105
'On his Blindness' (Sonnet XVI) 16, 25–6, 31–2
Orgel, Stephen 108

Paradise Lost 8, 14, 15–16, 17, 27, 35–43, 55–6, 58, 59–76, 77, 78–9, 81–4, 86–92, 95, 98
Paradise Regained 17, 43–5, 95–104
Parker, W.R. 106
plain style 13, 43
power 8–9, 14, 18, 57, 64–7, 68, 69, 71–4
presence 6, 14, 19–23, 24–26, 31, 34, 41, 43, 45, 68, 70
Prince, F.T. 35, 107
Prynne, William 110

Reason of Church Government, The 20
resistance 11, 72, 74
Revolution, the English 10–15, 17
Ricks, Christopher 34, 107, 108
Romantics 91–2

St Paul 47, 65, 78
Samson Agonistes 8, 16–17, 53–8, 59, 65, 93–5
Saussure, Ferdinand de 69
sexuality 53–8, 64–7
Shakespeare 27, 35, 88–9
Shelley, P.B. 91, 111
signifier 6–7, 11, 13, 20, 22, 23, 24, 35, 37, 38, 41–2, 43, 44–5, 65, 68–70, 74, 83, 105
Spenser, Edmund 35, 51, 86, 96
Stallybrass, Peter 106
Stubbes, Philip 110
subjectivity 7, 8, 25, 32, 33, 70, 73, 75, 76, 85–95
Sweezy, Paul 106